PETER LEMON

VERMONT BACKROADS

by Mollie Yoneko Matteson

American Geographic Publishing
Helena, Montana

William A. Cordingley, Chairman
Rick Graetz, Publisher
Mark Thompson, Director of Publications
Barbara Fifer, Production Manager

VERMONT GEOGRAPHIC SERIES

Number 2

Acknowledgments

It would have been impossible to write this book without the hospitality, support, and knowledge of backroads Vermont provided by Robert and Mary Matteson, and Ed and Brenda Orwe. Their help is deeply appreciated.

Dedication

And without my sisters—Brenda, Ruthie and Carol—all those bumpy, dusty rides wouldn't have been nearly as much fun. This book is dedicated to them.

Library of Congress Cataloging-in-Publication Data
Matteson, Mollie Yoneko.
  Vermont backroads / by Mollie Yoneko Matteson.
      p.   cm. -- (Vermont geographic series ; no. 2)
  Bibliography: p.
  ISBN 0-938314-50-5 (pbk.) : $15.95
  1. Vermont--Description and travel--1981- -- Tours. 2. Natural history--Vermont--Guide-
books. I. Title. II. Series.
F47.3.M37 1988
917.43'0443--dc19
                                                                        88-8149
                                                                          CIP

ISBN 0-938314-50-5

© 1988 American Geographic Publishing, P.O. Box 5630, Helena, MT 59604. All rights reserved.

text © 1988 Mollie Yoneko Matteson

Printed in Korea by Dong-A Printing Co.

DICK DIETRICH

PETER LEMON

DICK DIETRICH

DICK DIETRICH

Above: *Bogie farm at Peacham.*
Left top: *Howe Bridge in Tunbridge.*
Left: *Putney.*
Facing page, left: *Carpenter Hill Road.*
Right: *Windham County Courthouse, Newfane.*
Title page: *Between Danby and Four Corners.*
Front cover: *East Orange.* DICK DIETRICH

3

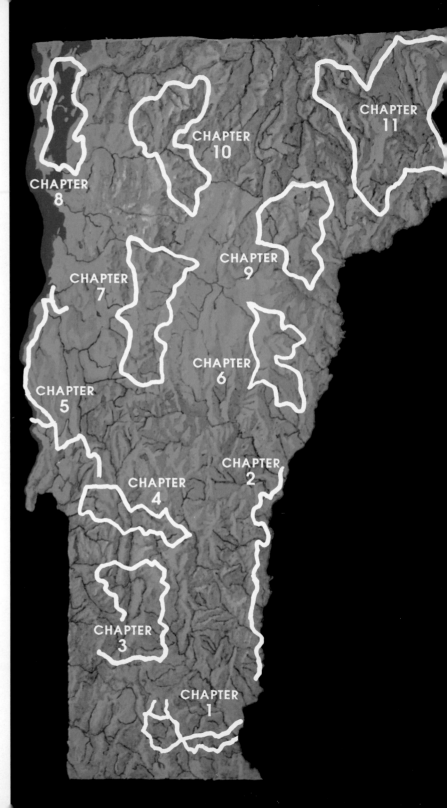

About the Author

Mollie Yoneko Matteson grew up in Southwestern Vermont, where her family's roots can be traced to the first settlers of the region. Her father's passion for driving "roads less traveled" acquainted her at an early age with backroads travel and lore. She has worked for the Vermont Parks Department, the National Park Service, the U.S. Forest Service, and as a free-lance writer. Her first book (co-authored with George Wuerthner)—*Vermont: Portrait of the Land and Its People*—was the first title in American Geographic Publishing's Vermont Geographic Series.

DICK DIETRICH

Above: *West Barnet.*
Facing page: *Roaring Branch in the Green Mountain National Forest.*

GEORGE WUERTHNER

CONTENTS

DICK DIETRICH

To a child, the road itself is the thing. When Dad steered the station wagon onto the dusty track, Mom's face hardened as she directed us to roll up all the windows. Dad liked the sense of adventure he felt driving backroads, and he liked the scenery. Mom liked the scenery, but not the dirt, or the possibility of a flat tire on some empty stretch of unpaved byway. My sisters and I were not interested in the scenery, nor the predictable human drama that unfolded between the two in the front seat. We just liked the ride.

It was usually stifling in the car, with windows shut tight against the clouds of summer road dust that swirled in our wake. The rumble of tires on loose gravel was loud and vaguely thrilling and the "washboarded" sections rattled our jaws. The best part, however, were the "thank-you-mum's" (my sisters and I called them sickening bumps) that left our stomachs suspended several inches above our heads. The car would roll down a long dip, then suddenly…up! Too many of them made me ill—like riding a roller coaster. But what kid doesn't love a roller coaster, even while it makes her turn green?

Out of these many childhood cruises of Vermont backroads my sense of adventure and my love of exploration developed. Eventually, I did become interested in the scenery, in the history of the countryside a road passes through, in the ways in which the landscape reveals an area's social and economic make-up. To me, the backroads of Vermont offer discovery, recreation, beauty *and* an education. Thus, this book attempts to expedite and enrich the quest for all these things, whether the reader is a newcomer or a native, a novice or a connoisseur of backroads.

The lost "flatlander" is notoriously the butt of native jokes, yet even the Vermonter born and raised can easily get "temporarily disoriented" in the tangle of roads haphazardly woven all over the state. Vermont has a wealth of travelways relative to other regions of the country, due to its long history and the changing social, economic and technological scene over the past several centuries. There are undoubtedly many

PETER LEMON

Left: "Ya can't get thar from here." So says an old Yankee farmer to a befuddled flatlander in a familiar Vermont joke. Attempting to navigate on the state's backroads can be a humbling experience.

Facing page: Peacham.

more abandoned tracks in Vermont today than there are roads in active use. And a large number of the latter are still unpaved byways and side roads that are little changed (and receive not much more traffic) from a hundred years ago. Problems for the traveler lie not merely in this sheer extravagance of roads, but also in the dearth of signs that either point the way, or even name the road. Also, the ordinary state highway map can only show a fraction of all the possible ways to travel from A to B. It would be unreadable if the mapmakers attempted a more complete picture.

Many Vermonters heat with wood, a relatively abundant resource in a state that is 80 percent forested. Waits River.

DICK DIETRICH

This is not a guidebook in the usual sense. The reader will not find every road mile intricately described, nor each turnoff point carefully pointed out. It is better imagined as a tour guide, directing the traveler's attention to the most interesting and attractive sights along the way. Background information is selectively provided; enough to enhance the experience, but not enough to make the reader an expert.

Before setting out, however, it will be helpful to have some general facts about Vermont in mind. Vermont is a small piece of land, about 9,609 miles square and 43rd in size among the 50 states. At its narrowest, Vermont is only about 40 miles across; at its widest, 90 miles. It is 158 miles long from the Canadian border to Massachusetts and bounded on either side by water: the Connecticut River separates it on the east from New Hampshire; Lake Champlain sits between Vermont and New York on the west side, for about three quarters of their shared border.

Resident Vermonters are relatively few in number as well. Approximately 535,000 people lived here in 1985, making the Green Mountain State 48th in population size. The largest city of Burlington claims only 38,000 inhabitants, though the greater Burlington area actually functions as a small metropolitan area, with some 82,000 residents. Greater Rutland was home to some 26,085 persons in 1980, and when the city and town populations of Barre are combined, they total about 16,900. Bennington is inhabited by about 16,000 people as well. Only three other towns have populations over 10,000.

Many Vermonters are rural dwellers, but of Vermont's total population, some 60 percent are "rural nonfarm," meaning people who live in the country, but do not obtain their livelihood from cultivating the land. They commute to work in larger population centers, probably driving part of the way on graveled roads. Or these rural dwellers may be writers, artists, retirees or independently wealthy.

Very real poverty exists on many backroads in the state, and many native Vermonters live in country homes that most picture books, postcards and the 1 million visitors a year tend to ignore. Pastoral architecture is as likely to be exemplified in shabby metal trailers and sagging shacks, as in restored colonial farmhouses and the cedar-and-glass angled boxes of the nouveau riche.

It is not impossible to stray from the beaten path, but it does require preparation as well as a willingness to not always know exactly where one is. In addition to the maps provided in this book, it would be wise for the serious backroader to obtain a state highway map as well as a Vermont road atlas (see Resources listing at back of book). Most tours described here follow routes shown on the official state map, but it will be easier to make correct decisions at intersections and turnoffs with a more detailed road map.

Beyond acreage and population statistics, Vermont is diminutive in other ways. The Green Mountains are not the Grand Tetons; the rolling farm country of northern Vermont is not the Midwest; the Lake Champlain lowlands are not the Great Plains. The peaks are not high; the flats are always reassuringly and closely bounded by hills or mountains.

The interweaving of natural and human landscapes in Vermont is quiet, modest and without fanfare. This is not to say that the result is not attractive. It is. And when light, weather and season converge in an exalted moment on scenes of field and forest, hill and village, lake and mountain, the effect leaves one breathless.

Vermont is divided into six physiographic regions: the Green Mountains, running north-south down the center of the state; the Taconic Mountains on the southwest border; the Valley of Vermont; the Champlain Lowlands adjacent to Lake Champlain; the Vermont Piedmont on the east side of the Green Mountains; and the Northeast Highlands.

The Green Mountains form a broad plateau at the southern end and narrow as they progress northward. Mt. Mansfield, the highest point in the state, stands at 4,393 feet above sea level. There are 99 other named peaks above 3,000 feet in the state, including a few in the Taconics and isolated peaks in the Vermont piedmont. The Taconics are generally lower than the Green Mountains, but are more broken and rugged. Between these lies the Valley of Vermont, running from approximately Bennington to just north of Rutland. This flat, straight stretch of lowland has been a travel corridor since the early human history of the region. The Champlain Lowland is a broader ribbon of ground between the lake and the Green Mountains; it is about 109 miles long from north of Rutland to the Canadian border. The Vermont Piedmont is a large region of hills that extends the length of the state, between the Green Mountains and the Connecticut River. In places higher peaks and intrusions of granite accent the generally subdued character of the terrain. The Northeast Highlands occupy the northeast corner of the state—their average elevation is high, but the topography is basically flat to rolling, with protruding bumps and knobs of granite. This is the most sparsely populated and wildest region of Vermont.

Vermont was spottily and intermittently settled during the first half of the 18th century, but not until the close of the

GEORGE WUERTHNER

French and Indian Wars in 1759 did the first true wave of settlement sweep over Vermont. Pioneers from the surrounding colonies of Massachusetts, Connecticut and New York came to Vermont.

This territory north of Massachusetts and between New York and New Hampshire was disputed ground for many decades. Vermont was called the New Hampshire Grants from about 1749—when New Hampshire governor Benning Wentworth took it upon himself to grant the first town of Bennington—to 1777, when the citizens of the Grants officially declared independence.

Although Wentworth was enthusiastic in his grant-making after settlement boomed in 1761, New York also

Backroads can take one through some of the wildest areas left in the state, as well as more pastoral settings. Beebe Pond in the Green Mountain National Forest.

9

claimed authority over the region west of the Connecticut River and petitioned the king of England to stop Wentworth's activities. By the time the king decided in favor of New York in 1764, Wentworth had granted 131 towns. New York made conflicting grants, and settlers under the Wentworth grants faced eviction as the New York courts did not recognize their claims. The residents of the Grants organized resistance against New York authority. Not all Grants citizens favored resistance, however. These "Tories" met with discrimination, or worse, at the hands of the Green Mountain Boys and others who favored independence for the disputed region. At the same time resistance to British rule was growing throughout the American colonies, except in New York. The hostility of the Grants inhabitants against the Yorkers became synonymous with their antipathy to British rule.

Ethan Allen, hero of the Green Mountain Boys, was most famous action for taking Fort Ticonderoga, a British stronghold on the New York side of Lake Champlain, in 1775. Also in 1775, the first of the series of conventions that would lead to the declaration of an independent Vermont met in Dorset. In 1776, the 4th Convention resolved to make application that the Grants be formed into a separate district.

Early in 1777, convention attendees declared the Grants an independent state, decided on the name of "Vermont" and adopted a constitution. The state thus was the first in history to grant the right to vote to all men, regardless of race or wealth, and the first to prohibit slavery in any form.

By 1780, the young American federation still refused to recognize Vermont as an independent state. In 1781, the war between Britain and the colonies concluded at Yorktown, and a resolution introduced in Congress to recognize Vermont did not pass. Vermont continued as a separate republic, with its own government and money, while New York and Massachusetts made claims on border towns and the state as a whole more desperately and aggressively than ever before. Finally, in 1790, New York relinquished its claims and in 1791 Vermont adopted the Constitution of the United States and was accepted into the Union as the 14th state.

During the next century, Vermont lost population as farm fertility declined and better agricultural lands opened up in the Midwest. The state did develop economically, however, and the importance of manufacturing grew. The railroads arrived at mid-century, stimulating industry and commerce, and bringing more visitors to the state.

The 20th century was slow to bring significant change to the state, at first. While the rest of the nation became increasingly urban and federal and state governments grew in strength and importance, Vermont stayed rural and its towns resolutely held on to their near-autonomy. The disastrous flood of 1927 prompted the change that inevitably had to come to Vermont's government. The natural catastrophe caused millions of dollars worth of damage, and the state was forced to apply for federal relief funds. The state government, empowered by the need for a central distributor and overseer of the monies, grew in importance and so changed Vermont politics forever.

Not until 1963, however, did Vermont elect its first Democratic governor since 1854. This signalled the lasting shift in Vermont demographics. Between 1960 and 1970, the state's population grew by 14 percent, a significant fraction of which was newcomers. A few decades before, Vermont had lost more people through emigration than it had gained through natural increase.

Many who came to live in Vermont did so because they wished to escape the ugliness and fast pace of more-urban settings. These new citizens tended to be more liberal than the native population; they were concerned about the environment, the preservation of the rural landscape, social and human services. They cherished Vermont for what it had been—a placid backwater—even as it changed, even as they brought with them the politics, attitudes and ways of life of the places they had left.

Today, all Vermonters recognize that their beloved state is changing rapidly and unavoidably. The backroads are being paved; more subdivisions are springing up, and houses—both year-round dwellings and second homes—dot the woods. More Vermonters work in manufacturing or the service industry. The few remaining farmers are struggling in an increasingly uneconomic business, in which the option of subdividing their own land or selling to developers is very tempting.

All Vermonters, whether they fight to keep some dirt road unpaved, or push for economic and industrial development in the state (it is conceivable that some people

GEORGE WUERTHNER

do both), feel loyalty to the Vermont "idea," hazy as that may be. Despite the intense debates that are now being waged between legislators, politicians, town leaders and neighbors across the fence, the rural and natural character of the state is important to every person in it. How Vermonters will decide to preserve their state is unsure, but one need only drive a few of its backroads to see why they would want to.

Preservation of Vermont's special "look" and character is a matter close to the heart of every resident. Near Guildhall.

11

GEORGE WUERTHNER

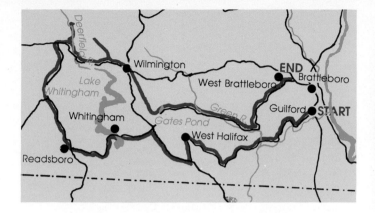

GUILDFORD, WHITINGHAM, READSBORO, WILMINGTON

It may surprise many Vermonters to learn that some of the wildest, least-trammeled ground in the state lies at its southern edge, along the Massachusetts border. No doubt, the northeastern corner is the most remote and extensive parcel of wild and semi-wild ground in Vermont, and it is widely celebrated for its primeval character. But few sing praises of the piece of land between Brattleboro and Bennington that takes in two sparsely populated hill towns and a completely unpeopled, highland wilderness.

Near its southern terminus, the Green Mountain Range broadens from a more well-defined ridgeline into a rolling, high plateau, dissected by narrow stream courses. It is easily apparent why few people have ever chosen to inhabit this rocky, swamp-dotted and mosquito-plagued tableland, which also receives greater amounts of snow, on the average, than the mountains to the north—due to its proximity to the Atlantic Ocean and winter storm tracks.

Less obvious is the reason the towns of Guilford and Halifax—which lie on the lower, undulant terrain to the east—are today marked only by a few pocket-size hamlets,

PETER LEMON

when in their early history they were bustling centers of commerce and hotbeds of political conflict.

For more than 20 years after the town was granted, Guilford, by terms of its charter, was answerable only to the King of England. In 1775 it joined with the other towns of Vermont, but a good number of Guilford's citizens did not find it easy to shift loyalties from the monarch of a world power to the seeming "mob rule" government of Vermont's rebels-turned-statesmen. Loyalist sentiments became public policy in Guilford when in 1782 "...the electorate met in general and voted to stand against the pretended State of Vermont." Vermont had already announced its independence, but nine years would pass before it was admitted as the 14th state in the union.

Not all Guilfordites favored the Mother Country, however, and a kind of civil war kept Guilford in chaos for several years. People attending town meeting often toted

Above: *Guilford's heyday passed two centuries ago.*

Facing page: *The high, undulating tableland of the southern Green Mountain Range never has been good ground for farming. Today it is more important for recreation—downhill and nordic skiing, snowmobiling, hiking and hunting—and as a source of hydroelectric power for out-of-state consumers. Guilford.*

13

The observant traveler will note, as at this West Guilford cemetery, that many hinterland communities have several times more dead people than living.

PETER LEMON

weapons; fights were frequent.perhaps the pro-monarchy, pro-Yorker faction and the pro-Yankee, pro-Vermont faction each hoped to resolve the matter by electing its own set of town officials. Eventually the state lost patience, and sent Ethan Allen and a force of militiamen to Guilford, where they collected taxes and enforced martial law. Most of the citizens who had stood against the "pretended state" believed enough in its hostility toward them to leave town and resettle in New York.

Despite this emigration, Guilford was the most populous town in Vermont in 1791, the year of statehood and the first statewide census. Of a total of 85,539 Vermonters, Guilford had 2,500; it was half again as large as any other town. Two things accounted for this density of humanity in a place far

from ideal for agriculture and efficient transportation. First, Guilford is only a few miles from the Connecticut River and lies on the Vermont-Massachusetts border: it was close to the people who wanted to move to the new frontier of Vermont. Second, the early proprietors were smart developers, and offered tempting land deals that stimulated rapid settlement and growth.

After the 1791 census, Guilford lost population for the subsequent 150 years. Much of the state stagnated as well during that period, but many communities recovered during the surge of growth that began in the 1960s and continues to the present. Guilford was among those that remained in the sticks. Today it has something more than 1,500 residents scattered among its several villages and upland farms and woods. It is difficult now to imagine any kind of tumult in this peaceful backwater. The same may be said of Halifax, Guilford's neighbor to the west, only more so. Halifax boasted a population of 1,500 in 1820, but has fewer than 500 people today.

From Guilford to Halifax and, on the return stretch of this tour, from Gates Pond to the outskirts of Brattleboro, this loop drive offers the purest kind of backroading. The bumpy, meandering, unpaved byways connect one "nowhere" to another "nothing much"; they feature no particularly significant historic site or breathtaking vista. They are simply—to the backroad connoisseur—delightful.

The up-and-down terrain that characterizes Guilford and Halifax is part of the Vermont piedmont. The western half of Halifax might be more properly identified as the edge of the Green Mountain massif, but on the east side of the range it is difficult to judge where the piedmont—or foothills—ends and the mountains begin. The land's incline from the Connecticut River to the rounded summits of the range is gradual, and the numerous swells in the topography are distracting.

One need not be a geologist, however, or have an altimeter along to recognize where one zone gives way to the next. Driving westward from the main village of Guilford, one notes that open meadows and farms become less frequent, and the forests grow denser and dimmer. In the mid-1800s, approximately 80 percent of the state was cleared for lumber and to create pastures for sheep and cattle. Today, the proportions are reversed, and farms survive only where the soils are richer and the local climates less extreme. The triumph of the trees is graphically demonstrated in the miles between Guilford and the village of Green River. Westward to Halifax, the road climbs and the forest is in command. Here and there a rustic cabin, most of them apparently hunting or summer camps, may be glimpsed through the trees.

Before the road descends to the village of Halifax, a few rather leaf-obscured views reveal the mountains to the south in Massachusetts. The Berkshires are really an extension of the Green Mountains and, like them, are essentially level, with a few rounded protrusions. Also, like the southern Green Mountains, this section of northern Massachusetts is thinly peopled and economically stalled.

This monument to Brigham Young at Whitingham is like a transported fragment of the kingdom he was to build in Utah's desert.

GEORGE WUERTHNER

From West Halifax to Jacksonville, the road, now paved, follows a couple of tributaries to the North River. After the hamlets of Halifax, Jacksonville seems a regular metropolis. Actually, it is only a surprisingly well maintained mountain town, uncommercialized and made gracious by several large homes. Route 100 splits here, one fork heading north to Wilmington, the other aimed for the village of Whitingham, birthplace of religious leader Brigham Young.

Atop Town Hill, a tall stone monument to Young stands at the edge of a meadow. It faces west, appropriately, for it was Young, along with another Vermont son, Joseph Smith, who led the fledgling Mormon church westward to Utah in the mid-19th century. Born in 1801, Young received

15

The Deerfield River, which eventually reaches the Connecticut River (in Massachusetts), once served as a transportation corridor for logs cut from the southern Green Mountains.

only two months of formal education, yet proved himself a brilliant social and religious organizer. Husband to 70 wives and father to 56 children, the polygamist Young was also a man of "superb equipment", as another marker at his actual birth site proclaims.

On the hilltop where Brigham Young came into the earthly world, a long vista to the north invites admiration. Lake Whitingham—also known as Harriman Reservoir

because it is impounded by the Harriman Dam—fills a trough in the midst of rounded mountains. This reservoir and another in Searsburg produce hydropower, none of it utilized by Vermont consumers. Throughout Vermont, hydro provides for 20 percent of the state's electrical energy needs.

In earlier days, the Deerfield River powered a paper mill and a chair factory in Readsboro. Historical photographs show a busy mountain town in the latter half of the 19th century:

PETER LEMON PHOTOS BOTH PAGES

long strings of flatbeds, piled high with logs; railroad yards crowded with logs, engines and men. The golden age of logging and railroading was long ago, however, and tired-looking Readsboro seems a place the world passed by. Nothing is new in Readsboro, and everything that is old—the steepled church, the clapboard houses lining the main street, the village gazebo—seems to have been neglected for many decades.

Nowhere else is the disparity between poverty and wealth, archaic industry and contemporary resources, between the forgotten Vermont towns and the chic upcountry destinations, so clear as in the state's mountains. North and east of Readsboro is the resort town of Wilmington, which, like other major ski areas in Vermont, did not really boom until the 1950s and 1960s. Before Wilmington became hot real estate, and its tiny downtown village packed with boutiques and stylish eateries, it was—like Readsboro—a farming, then a logging, center. When farming, then logging,

faltered in the harsh, hard-to-reach highlands, Readsboro and its sister towns—Stamford, Woodford, Searsburg—declined in population and prosperity. The poorest mountain hamlets disappeared altogether. Wilmington could have seen a similar fate but for easier access via Route 9, proximity to some large, accessible mountain slopes and a developer's scheme. Wilmington followed the upward curve of the recreation and tourist industry, now the second-largest component of the Vermont economy.

Between Readsboro and Wilmington, several rewarding side trips can be made to interesting natural features of the southern mountain plateau. Howe Pond, north of Readsboro and off Route 100, is encircled by state forest and can be reached by an unimproved dirt road. Boggy edges and wet woods make an intriguing high-elevation wetland, and blooming wild azaleas are a special attraction in the spring.

In Searsburg, the turnoff to Somerset Reservoir can be followed all the way to this very beautiful, undeveloped lake.

Above: In contrast to ever-busy Wilmington, the hamlet of Green River moves so slowly, a covered bridge doubles as a post office.

Left: The Mount Snow ski area largely is responsible for Wilmington's initial entry into resort status. It is now a popular year-round destination.

GEORGE WUERTHNER

PETER LEMON

A more strenuous option is to hike the trail that starts about 2 miles beyond Route 9, on the east side of the road. It is approximately 5 miles to the lake by this route, which follows the East Branch of the Deerfield River, past beaver ponds and through forests of white pine and northern hardwoods.

Another diversion for hikers is the short but steep trail up Haystack Mountain, from the grassy summit of which there are views of Mount Greylock—the highest point in Massachusetts—and Mount Monadnock in New Hampshire. The access road to the trailhead leads northward from the intersection of Routes 9 and 100 in Wilmington.

PETER LEMON

Left: *Readsboro, once the hub of a vigorous logging and wood products industry, today is a forgotten corner of the state.*

Facing page, left: *False hellebore is common in moist areas, of which there is an abundance in the poorly drained soils of the southern Green Mountains.*
Right: *Sadawga Pond in Whitingham is noted for its "floating island"—in reality a tangled mat of vegetation.*

To reach Gates Pond, another natural area featuring grassy wetlands and a rich wildlife community, the more cautious traveler can take Route 100 south to Jacksonville, then turn left, northbound, on a secondary paved road. The pavement continues until the pond is reached. The adventurous backroader should stay on Route 9 just a mile or so east of the intersection with southbound Route 100. An unimproved dirt road to the right turns south to wind through the Wilmington Town Forest and within a few miles meets with the paved road described above. Past Gates Pond, the way is again rougher, more remote, and where it begins to follow the lovely Green River, more classically "backroadish." Only a few cabins tucked under the dark eastern hemlocks belie a human presence in the dim and narrow river bottom. Metamorphic rocks of the Vermont piedmont crop out alongside the road—furred in moss and green-gray lichens. As the stream descends towards the Connecticut River, the woods thin and more signs of human habitation appear.

19

DICK DIETRICH

PUTNEY TO WHITE RIVER JUNCTION

In 1760, southern New England had no more room for its young people. America in the 18th century was an agrarian society; the vast majority of people lived a subsistence lifestyle, obtaining food, fiber, building materials and fuel from the land they owned and worked. Not incidentally, land yielded the rights of citizenship as well. And when no arable land remained to be cleared by young farmers in the colonies of Massachusetts, Connecticut and Rhode Island, they were forced to find new frontiers. The West was still unknown, unexplored, unreachable. Instead, the pioneers looked to the wilderness to their north.

During the French and Indian Wars—a protracted struggle between the French and the British (and their respective Indian allies)—Vermont had been a kind of no-man's land through which raiding parties traveled to reach objectives on the lower Connecticut, on Lake Champlain or in Canada. Colonists, still under British rule, were enlisted in the military campaigns and in projects such as the construction of the Crown Point Military Road. In this way, young men from southern New England were able to view this virtually unknown territory of the Green Mountains. When the war ended late in 1759 with the British capture of Quebec, the men went home to tell their families and neighbors of the land they had seen. Over the next decade, settlers poured into Vermont.

The Connecticut River was a natural entry to the Green Mountain frontier, and some of the earliest settlement occurred along its shores and in the adjoining foothills. Most original pioneers in the region had been residents of the Connecticut Valley further downstream; they simply emigrated upriver. Similarly, western New Englanders headed due north for the Valley of Vermont and the Champlain Valley.

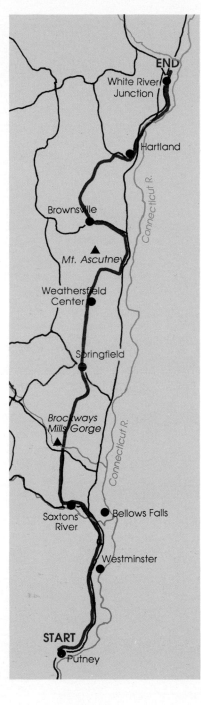

PETER LEMON

Above: *Putney's fertile, flat river benches attracted settlers early in the region's history.*

Facing page: *Scenes such as this in Pomfret typify the subdued nature of the landscape on the Vermont piedmont, between the Green Mountain Range and the Connecticut River.*

GEORGE WUERTHNER

Where it forms the boundary between Vermont and New Hampshire, the Connecticut is not an impressively large river, nor is its valley notably broad. In glacial ages, sheets of continental ice gouged the valley deeper and wider, but their retreat left behind enormous quantities of sediment. In the hills bordering the river valley, these deposits were mostly glacial till—an unsorted mixture of boulders and smaller rocks. In the lowland, meltwater collected and formed one large lake, or perhaps a series of several smaller lakes. Drainage to the north was blocked by the terminal end of the retreating glacier, and at the southern end, by piles of rocky glacial debris called moraines. The streams which flowed into the lake delivered not only water, but as in lakes today, contributed loads of sediment which settled to the bottom. Unlike the till on the uplands, these deposits were composed of very fine particles, distributed evenly over the lake bottom in horizontal layers. The lake bottom sediments are evident today, albeit in fragmented form, as the bands and lobes of flat, fertile river terraces along the sides of the valley. The finest farmland on this side of the state is to be found on these Connecticut River benches.

At Putney, where this tour begins, the river twists into two prominent bows. The River Road off Route 5, just north of the main village, leads across both. The curving riverbanks cup broad fields—fields cleared very early, some time before New Hampshire Governor Benning Wentworth granted the town of Putney in 1753. In fact, a fortification was built here in 1742 in order to deter Indian raids on Massachusetts communities to the south.

The farms on the eastern border of the state occupy a thin ribbon of still-profitable land. Most agriculture in the state now occurs in the counties bordering Lake Champlain and, to a lesser extent, the rolling terrain surrounding Lake Memphremagog. Yet profitable farming does survive elsewhere in Vermont, in scattered pockets of good land, as proved by the relatively hale-looking operations seen along this drive.

Agricultural endeavor, of course, once reached the highest hilltops and across the poorest, rocky soils in the state. In 1811, William Jarvis, consul to Portugal, brought several thousand Spanish Merino sheep to his farm on Weathersfield Bow—another fat crescent of river terrace on the

Left: *Vermont's sheep era reached its peak more than 150 years ago, but the woolies still are kept by a significant number of part-time farmers. The interest now is primarily in supplying meat to regional markets, but Vermont wool has developed a special cachet, and market, as well.*

Facing page: *Into the old shops lining Putney's downtown streets have moved artisans and young entrepreneurs, making for a lively business district that also is visually appealing.*

Connecticut. The hardy woolies, well suited to the northern New England climate, thrived even on the boulder-plagued hills that would support no other crop but trees. Spurred by a growing textile industry in southern New England, wool became king in Vermont for the next 20 years. The old adage that Vermont has more cows than people was always a myth. But at one time, there were six sheep to every person. Windsor County, through which this backroad tour passes, was one of the leading sheep counties in the state.

Sheep are not picky eaters. They will graze just about anything, which is why they did so well on Vermont's uplands, and why those rocky slopes suffered not only the insult of deforestation, but the ravages of overgrazing as well. Without a cover of trees, nor much of any other kind of vegetation to hold back the soil, erosion was severe in many places and floods increased in frequency and intensity. The fertility of croplands diminished as the valuable topsoil was washed away.

By the 1830s, sheep-raising reached its peak in Vermont, and the industry gradually declined. Dairy farming, which required better, more-productive land, had no use for the upland meadows, which were abandoned. The trees slowly

Satisfied customers of a "you-pick" berry farm in Putney are testimony to the region's fertility and ideal situation for fruit growing.

PETER LEMON

returned. Although the higher hills and Mountainsides are likely to remain forested for the foreseeable future, a few lower, favorably situated slopes have been maintained or reclaimed for another kind of crop: apples. Vermont is not a significant producer of apples, when considered on a national basis, but orchards are locally important, and certainly lend appeal to the landscape—particularly during the spring blossoming. At the town of Putney, one tenth of Vermont's apples are grown. The orchards drape across slopes facing the Connecticut. They are planted on the sides of the valley, rather than on the valley floor, because heavy cold air sinks to the valley bottom, and the slopes above are actually warmer by several degrees. Even slight differences in temperature can determine whether or not a crop will fail.

Putney has provided fertile ground for innovative thinking, too. During the early to mid-19th century, an era of Utopian ideals and spiritual revival gave birth to new religions and "counterculture" experiments throughout the country. Vermont in general seems to have been rife with them, and Putney was involuntary host to one called Perfectionism, in which communal living included sharing not only property, but wives as well. This enlightened way of life was not appreciated by all the townsfolk and, after a tenure of nine years, John Humphrey Noyes, leader of the group, was charged with adultery and forced to flee the area. The Perfectionists eventually settled in at Oneida, New York, where they founded the famous silverware company that managed to outlive their social experiment.

The River Road eventually rejoins Route 5 and leads toward the historic town of Westminster. Today Westminster is a relatively peaceful place, but in the late 18th century it was the site of several key events in the struggle for Vermont independence. The gracious, broad highway that arrows down the middle of the village of Westminster, for example, was originally a military training ground.

In 1768, New York divided Vermont, over which it claimed jurisdiction, into several large counties. In each it established shiretowns, or county seats, where the county courts—presided over by New York appointees—were located. Cumberland County encompassed the general area that are now Windham and Windsor counties in the southeast corner of the state. Although Chester was originally the shiretown of Cumberland County, New York officials decided to rename Westminster the seat of county government in 1772. Apparently Chester harbored a great deal of resistance to New York authority.

Unfortunately for the New Yorkers, Westminster citizens did not turn out to be any more cooperative. In 1774, they hosted a convention at which they declared that, as British subjects, they would defend their "just rights...against every foreign power that should attempt to deprive them of those rights..." Clearly, New York was considered a foreign power.

Early in the following year, a band of Westminster farmers attempted to prevent New York from holding court there, as they feared foreclosures on their properties. The

The Vermont Historical Railroad in Bellows Falls offers rides along the Connecticut River and recalls the golden age of the steam engine in Vermont.

rebels occupied the Westminster courthouse. Armed Yorker authorities confronted the angry crowd, and in the melee one Vermonter was killed, another fatally wounded and four were injured. Word of the "Westminster Massacre" spread quickly and, within two days, 500 agitated compatriots arrived. The New York sheriff, his men and court officers including the judge were thrown into jail.

Before the massacre, the east side and west side of the Grants had been somewhat divided in their commitment to the cause of Vermont independence and opposition to New York control. East-side residents were traditionally more Loyalist, more pro-British in their sentiments than the west-siders, among whom Ethan Allen and the "Bennington Mob" held sway. However, after the martyrdom of two east-side citizens, the territory became better unified in its stand against the common enemy. Two years later at Westminster, the sixth convention of Vermont declared it a free and independent state. And a year after that, the newborn republic got its first newspaper, the *Green Mountain Post Boy*, from this vigorous Connecticut River town.

Springfield.

before Vermont itself had much industry, raw materials such as wool, grain and lumber were floated downriver, and finished goods from southern New England were shipped up. Later, the ready transportation, as well as water power, stimulated manufacturing along the eastern border. Bellows Falls was the first place in the nation where paper was successfully made from wood pulp instead of cloth rags. Besides its importance in paper manufacturing, Bellows Falls also produced farm machinery, ammunition and silk.

Pleasant Valley Road climbs into the hills as it aims north for the next major tributary to the Connecticut, the Williams River. The village of Rockingham is situated on the Williams a short distance downstream from where the road intersects Route 103. The 200-year-old meeting house there is a well-known Vermont landmark, noted for its old New England design.

The tour route crosses the Williams River at Brockways Mills Gorge, a striking chasm through which the water roils and winds past vertical walls of rock overhung by dark green hemlocks. A dramatic look into the gorge rewards walkers along the railroad tracks that cross the road and lead to a bridge spanning the stream. Walking out on the bridge is not recommended, especially for those with a proclivity for vertigo.

The Brockways Mills Road from here climbs up again onto the piedmont, and affords occasional views of more distant uplands. Before the road begins its descent into Springfield, it passes Cobble Hill, whence came cobblestones for street paving in the days before macadam. These glacially deposited rocks were put to other uses as well, namely to build rock walls. Most modern farmers keep livestock in their pastures with barbed wire or wooden fencing, but rocks once were a kind of blessing when it came to constructing walls, although certainly cursed at many other times. With a plentiful supply of building materials at hand, farmers left enduring monuments to their labor alongside almost every backroad across the state's higher ground. Although long neglected and gradually succumbing to gravity, the lichen-encrusted stone fences are among the most ubiquitous Vermont traits.

Springfield is another manufacturing town with a long history. Today a town of 10,000, it began as the jump-off

Before leaving Westminster, travelers can make fruitful stops at the historical markers in Westminster village and at the small Westminster Historical Society museum. More views of the river appear before one reaches the turnoff that leads to the interstate. A secondary road parallels the four-laner north to the town of Rockingham.

The backroad route to the village of Saxtons River bypasses the major community of Bellows Falls, but a side trip to this key, industrial Connecticut river town is worthwhile. Indians used to come to the falls here—one of the biggest on the entire river—and fish for salmon. White men built the first bridge across the Connecticut here in 1785. (It was replaced by a steel version in 1905.) The first canal in the nation was constructed around the falls in 1802, and allowed boats to reach points north up to Wells River. The Connecticut became an increasingly important waterway;

PETER LEMON PHOTOS BOTH PAGES

Weathersfield Center is perhaps one of the brightest gems among the state's many backroads hamlets.

EFFIN OLDER

Right: The Ascutney Mountain Resort in Brownsville is a $50 million, 10-year development project—in which this 150-unit condominium hotel is only the first phase.

Facing page: Schist, perhaps the most common rock type in Vermont, is well exposed in Quechee Gorge.

point for the Crown Point Military road, which was constructed at the close of the French and Indian Wars to connect the fort at Charlestown, New Hampshire to Crown Point on Lake Champlain. The falls on the Black River, which flows through the heart of downtown Springfield, attracted mills early on. Later, they became the focus of several of the largest manufacturing firms in the state. Springfield became the capital of "machine tools"—machines that make machines. The industry brought Polish and Russian immigrants to work in the shops, and today this ethnic diversity subtle influences the community.

Precision Valley, as the Springfield area is known, is well endowed with large homes and a business district that speak of better days. In recent years, many of the town's

manufacturers have been either bought by out-of-state investors, or have left altogether. Firms located here since before the turn of the century can no longer compete in a market that has become international and that now includes formidable rivals like the Japanese.

On again to the uplands, and the ridgetop village of Weathersfield Center, from which a grand vista opens to the west through the branches of feral roadside apple trees. A thousand feet below lies the valley of the Black River; looming beyond, Hawks Mountain commands the near distance. Looking even farther, generally to the southwest, one finds a vision of spaciousness—so rare in this part of the state—unfolding. Gentle, undulating ground rolls gradually up to the Green Mountains, silhouetted on the horizon.

The deep-red brick, two-story meetinghouse presides with characteristic grace and stoicism over this hilltop hamlet. Nearby, the Reverend Dan Foster House is a fine example of a gracious colonial home, now restored and open to the public. Standing adjacent is the Old Forge, where a working forge and bellows may be seen. The Civil War memorial that stands in Weathersfield Center is not unusual—sculptured Union soldiers stonily survey many a Vermont village green, and an engraved plaque or carved marker is usually inscribed with the town's "Honor Roll." But, the 136 men who served from this town are believed to represent the highest proportion of native sons contributed to the cause, for any town in the Union states. In fact, Vermont granted a greater fraction of its men to the Union banner than almost any state in the nation, with close competition from Michigan and Kansas. Approximately 95 percent of those Green Mountain men were volunteers.

Mt. Ascutney begins a relatively steep climb up to its 3,144' summit on Weathersfield's northern border. Though not high, even by Vermont's rather modest standards, Ascutney is an arresting landmark here where it rises out of a sea of hills, most less than 1,500'. Ascutney is a monadnock, as are Burke Mountain near Lyndon and Mt. Monadnock near the western border of New Hampshire. These solitary prominences are composed of granite, a more resistant, harder rock than the types surrounding them. The monadnock rock is also younger: the rocks of Mt. Ascutney are 120 million years old, while the piedmont bedrock is three to four times older. Far below the earth's surface the monadnocks began as bodies of magma, or molten rock, which intruded into the pre-existing rocks. The magma squeezed through cracks and into larger, empty pockets. There it solidified, and as the softer rocks above and around it eroded slowly away, they exposed the body of harder rock to the surface. These local prominences are a crude measure of the amount of erosion the region has experienced.

During the age of glaciation, advancing ice sheets plucked rocks from Ascutney's summit and carried them southward. Later, as the glaciers melted, they dumped their load of rocks. Because Mt. Ascutney is one kind of rock, and the surrounding terrain another, geologists can trace this "train" of alien rocks and determine the path of the glaciers.

KEN LAYMAN; ROBERT MAUST PHOTOGRAPHY

29

ROBERT C. SIMPSON

Rocks originating from Ascutney have been found as far south as Massachusetts, more than 60 miles away.

A paved road and several hiking trails in Ascutney State Park lead to views of the Connecticut River valley and the Vermont piedmont. At one time a summit house stood atop the peak, accommodating 19th century vacationers who sought relief from the summer heat. Such structures perched on a number of Vermont Mountaintops: Killington, Mt. Mansfield, Camels Hump, Breadloaf Mountain, Mt. Equinox, Mt. Anthony in Bennington and Snake Mountain in Addison.

Modern recreationists come, not to ride up in carriages and lounge on breezy verandas, but instead to ride ski lifts up the northwest slopes of Ascutney in order to schuss back down to the base lodge and slope-side condominiums. Once a rather sleepy hamlet, the village of Brownsville only recently has been transformed to a multi-million-dollar resort, complete with hotel, restaurants, conference facilities and a sports and health center.

From the slopes north of Brownsville, the striped Mountainside of Ascutney dominates the scenery, particularly in winter when the snow-packed trails contrast with dark woods. Northward to Hartland Four Corners, the typical piedmont byway winds along the hilltops. The road follows Lulls Brook to the main village of Hartland, where the Sumner-Steele house is an excellent example of Georgian architecture. David Sumner, a prominent citizen, built the home in 1804.

Back on Route 5, one sees river-terrace farms spread beside the Connecticut. Its tributary, the Ottauquechee River, joins the main stream at North Hartland. A few miles upstream on the Ottauquechee, the river squeezes through the rugged defile of Quechee Gorge, 160' deep. Much like the Williams River that tumbles through Brockways Mills Gorge, the Ottauquechee cut the steep-walled canyon in a metamorphic rock called schist. This rock is characteristically ragged-looking and bears vague layers, usually contorted and tilted. In addition to its geological features, Quechee Gorge also hosts a small area of untouched mixed forest (rare in the East) with many boreal forest species.

White River Junction marks the convergence of two interstates (I-91 and I-89), Routes 5, 4 and 14, and railroad

494

PETER LEMON

lines whose days of glory now are gone. The White River and the Connecticut also meet here, and down both these streams great log rafts floated until 1900.

These streams have served as travel corridors not only for humans and their cargo but for wild creatures as well. The Connecticut River drainage once supported one of the largest runs of sea-going, or anadromous, fish in North America. The runs were an important food source for Indians and wildlife. The American shad swam up only as far as Bellows Falls, where the waterfall blocked its passage farther upstream. The Atlantic salmon continued nearly to Canada, and swam up side-streams to spawn. Born in freshwater streams, salmon swim to sea to feed and mature. At three to four years of age, salmon return to the streams where they were born, traveling hundreds of miles to mate and spawn.

Dam construction on the Connecticut, which began as early as the late 18th century, blocked the salmon's passage upriver. Moreover, the Atlantic salmon in general is heavily fished, and as much as 50 percent of the Connecticut's potential run is netted at sea. Still, since 1967, private power companies have cooperated with state and federal agencies to restore the Atlantic salmon to the Connecticut River drainage. This effort includes the construction of fish ladders to allow passage around the dams, as well as spawning habitat improvement and restocking. Recently, the White River welcomed back a few hardy fish, and it is hoped that the runs will reach points further up the drainage every year.

Left: *White River Junction once was the hub of several converging railroad lines. Today it serves interstate travelers.*

Facing page: *Quechee Gorge harbors a small boreal forest plant community, in which the pink lady's-slipper typically is found.*

GEORGE WUERTHNER PHOTOS BOTH PAGES

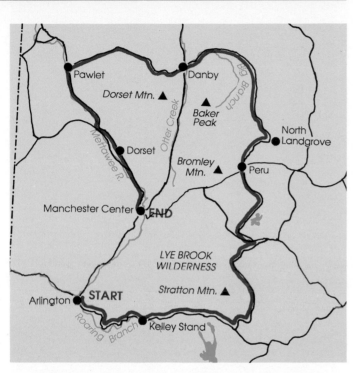

ARLINGTON, PERU, MOUNT TABOR, DANBY AND DORSET

Kelley Stand was a logging camp. High in the Green Mountains, this one east of Arlington on the boulder-packed Roaring Branch was like the dozens of other busy but fleeting settlements that sprang up in the densely wooded Vermont highlands in the 19th century. Strong men wielding axes, later saws, cut the hemlock, pine, spruce and fir, and skidded fat logs out across snow or iced roads. Some camps—or "jobs" as they were called—like Grout Job east of Kelley Stand got their logs to market by floating them downriver. At the job site, the loggers dammed streams, along which they piled the logs accumulated from a winter's work. In the spring, after the ice had melted, they opened the sluiceways and away rushed

the water with its cargo. Logs floated down the Deerfield River to paper mills, furniture mills and sawmills as far south as Holyoke, Massachusetts. Trees cut on the west side of the mountains were more likely skidded out individually down logging roads, although some ambitious railways scaled the mountainsides in Glastenbury in 1872 and Manchester in 1913.

Hardwoods like maple, beech and yellow birch were too to float out, but local charcoal kilns transformed the trees into of fuel for iron smelters. In southwest Vermont, for example, iron ore was mined in Bennington, Shaftsbury, Glastenbury and Stamford.

Later, the railroads demanded huge quantities of wood fuel, until the 1880s, when wood was replaced by anthracite and, later, bituminous coal. Lumber production in Vermont reached its height in the late 1880s. (Some 384 million board

Above: *Forests come back quickly in Vermont. Although the big trees of the virgin woods are gone, the thickness of the vegetation (including this hobblebush in bloom) seems to defy any ambition to keep the forests cleared for long.*

Facing page: *The Kelley Stand road parallels the hemlock-draped Roaring Branch to the crest of the Green Mountains.*

GEORGE WUERTHNER

PETER LEMON

Above: *Otter Creek and the Green Mountains near North Dorset.*
Right: *The Appalachian Trail and Vermont's Long Trail are one and the same along the Green Mountain's southern crest.*

feet were cut in 1889.) As trees disappeared, so did loggers and logging camps. Kelley Stand was gradually reclaimed by the same wilderness it—temporarily—had subdued. Today only a few scattered cellar holes mark where the old job once stood.

The Kelley Stand road connects two poor hamlets on either side of the southern Green Mountain range. Mostly unpaved, and closed to traffic in winter, the drive between Kansas on the west side and Stratton on the east is beautiful and wild. Several fine hiking trails in this part of the state—including Vermont's border-to-border Long Trail—take off from the roadside into a wilderness of dense northern

hardwood forest, numerous ponds and cascading streams. From the summits of 3,936' Stratton Mountain or 3,748' Glastenbury Mountain, a hiker may view one of the greatest expanses of undisturbed, natural landscape anywhere in Vermont outside the northeast corner. at the top of Stratton Mountain, Benjamin MacKaye conceived the idea for the Appalachian Trail and, in 1909, James Taylor was waiting for the mist to clear from the summit when he formulated the notion of a footpath through Vermont's wilderness, from "end to end." The 263-mile Long Trail was completed in 1931.

Although the sea of trees below these peaks may seem serenely lonely, the area accommodates thousands of

34

Bog near Beebe Pond.

GEORGE WUERTHNER

recreationists each year. Most of the territory is now within the borders of the Green Mountain National Forest. The 14,300-acre Lye Brook Wilderness and adjacent Stratton Pond on the Long Trail, are among the most frequent destinations for Green Mountain hikers, and hidden from view on Stratton Mountain's northeast face is one of the biggest ski resorts in the state.

Although today Stratton has not many more than 100 year-round residents, on a historic day in 1840, the population of Stratton township exceeded 15,000. The famed orator and statesman Daniel Webster led a political rally for the Whig party in the meadows at the base of Stratton Mountain, and attracted thousands of listeners. The site marker stands about two miles west of the Stratton Mountain trailhead; today only a small clearing survives the re-invasion of the forest.

The diminutive, tidy village of Peru sits just north of Route 11. Thousands of skiers and fall leaf peepers traverse the wild highlands via this stretch of highway, but far fewer take the narrow byway through Peru—a town with a name either ambitious or whimsical—and follow the ridgetops

GEORGE WUERTHNER

ROBERT C. SIMPSON

Above: *Looking west from the summit of Baker Peak, to the uplands of Danby and the Taconic Mountains.*
Right: *Northern flying squirrel, an inhabitant of dense coniferous and mixed forests.*

north to the even more remote town of Mount Tabor. Peru is surprisingly uncommercialized, despite its proximity to some of the largest ski areas in the state.

A few miles north of the village, Hapgood Pond Recreation area is a pleasant swimming and picnicking spot. Named for a family prominent in local history, the pond honors Marshall J. Hapgood, state legislator, land owner and an early player in the effort to establish Green Mountain National Forest.

The national forest system was established in 1905. Not long afterwards, Marshall Hapgood offered to sell some of his holdings cheaply to the federal government. Hapgood, who logged his own timberlands, was distressed by forestry practices of the time, and hoped to promote wiser, long-term

management of the land through establishment of a national forest in Vermont. At the time, however, Congress had not authorized government purchase of private land for the forest system. This was unfortunate for Vermont, where every acre had lain in private hands since 1793. The Weeks Act of 1911 did give the federal government authority to buy private land, but not until 1932 did the Green Mountain National Forest finally become a reality, and Hapgood's property became one of the first acquisitions.

Although many independent-minded Vermonters opposed the national forest idea initially, many were eventually convinced by two intensifying demands: for sound land management and for outdoor recreation opportunities in the densely populated eastern U.S. Although farming and logging had declined for several decades, the state still had only 64 percent forest cover—much of it growth. Decades of erosion had steepened drainages and already washed away water-absorptive topsoil. The flood of 1927, perhaps the greatest natural disaster Vermont ever experienced, was exacerbated by the lack of adequate vegetative cover on the fragile mountainsides. Forward-thinking persons of the time also predicted the need for naturally maintained public land for an increasingly urban population. Today some 50 million people live within a day's drive of the Green Mountain National Forest.

GEORGE WUERTHNER

MOLLIE MATTESON

The Forest Service has acquired about 50 percent of the area within the national forest borders, but finds it increasingly difficult to purchase private lands because of local opposition and competition from land developers. Unlike any other state in the nation, Vermont gives towns authority to veto proposed sales within their jurisdictions. The towns receive from the federal government 25 percent of the Forest Service gross receipts for logging, recreation and grazing fees. However, taxes from private development often promise much more revenue than this, and town boards of selectmen often must weigh local and immediate gains against the long-term benefits to a more amorphous "general public."

North Landgrove is one such island of private own-ership within the forest boundaries, but its charm is undeni-ably a public boon. The tiny township covers only 6,000 acres, compared to the 24,000 acre average of Vermont towns. Apparently, the first settler in what is now Landgrove thought he was in Peru. After hacking a homestead out of the wilder-ness, he discovered he was not in Peru, or any other granted township. The legislature complied with his request for a grant.

In the 1930s, Landgrove seemed destined to become a highland ghost town, like others in the southern mountains or in the northeast corner of the state. Landgrove, however, was saved from the trees and from complete obscurity by a few dedicated residents who lovingly preserved this piece of old New England. At this elevation, the open meadows are an anomaly, as are the well maintained properties some distance from any ski resort or large population center.

One building, situated on the left side of the road as one approaches the hamlet of North Landgrove from the west, is worthy of note. This house, attached to a series of sheds and barns behind it, was built with the harshness of New England winters in mind, and allowed its residents to do the farm chores and tend the animals without venturing into the often-hostile outside elements. This early architectural style is common in eastern Vermont, but rarely seen west of the Green Mountains. It is common in central and eastern Connecticut from where most of the pioneers to eastern Vermont came. Interestingly, many barns in southwest Vermont—and in that part of the state alone—exhibit a

Above: *The Yankee's answer to harsh New England winters: a farm where you never have to go outside.*
Left: *Peru.*

JAMES SCHWABEL

Views of the Dorset Inn, where early Vermont statesmen (and rabblerousers) met to determine the course of their controversial territory.

GEORGE WUERTHNER

Dutch architectural style. Because of the region's proximity to New York (which was first settled largely by the Dutch), southwest Vermont received both Dutch cultural ideas and styles, and actual Dutch pioneers.

This backroads route now swerves to the northwest on Danby Truck Trail Number 10, built by the Civilian Conservation Corps in the 1930s. Eventually, the route intersects the Long Trail, recently descended from the summits that dominate the western half of Peru and nearly the entire town of Mount Tabor. From Bromley Peak—swaddled in ski runs and lifts—north to Styles, Peru, Baker and Buckball Peaks, the footpath is rugged, steep and rewarding. Baker Peak in particular, also approachable from a trail winding up its western flank, offers invigorating prospects of the Valley of Vermont and the bulky, dark mass of Dorset Mountain, which squats almost too close for comfort across the narrow Valley of Vermont.

The forests of Mount Tabor made Vermont's first millionaire early in this century. Silas Griffith owned sawmills,

lumber yards and charcoal plants in the village of Mount Tabor, which eventually became known as Griffith. So much a company town was this, every road or trail or stream had a mill, and each was labeled "S.L. Griffith" on maps of the day. Only the ruins of a few brick charcoal kilns testify to the former existence of Silas Griffith's empire. At the base of Dorset Mountain, outcrops of contorted, whitish-gray rock hint at the subsurface composition. A core of marble has made the mountain an important quarry site since the 1840s. The Imperial Quarry, its entrance at 1,690' on the side of the 3,804' peak, is now the premier producer of marble in Vermont. Annual production is 200,000 cubic feet and the subsurface quarry covers 20 acres. Giant pillars evenly spaced support the roof. The Vermont Marble Company, which owns the Imperial, claims it is the largest underground marble quarry in the world.

The marble lies in horizontal layers, buried under nine feet of overburden, which must be stripped off before the

Near Danby, in the Taconic Mountains.

GEORGE WUERTHNER

marble itself is taken. Dynamite would shatter the fragile rock, so workers drill holes both horizontally and vertically, then drive wedges into the holes until the marble splits off. Blocks normally five feet by eight feet and weighing 18 tons are transported to the Vermont Marble Company's processing center in Proctor.

The road to Danby Four Corners climbs through the stream-cut ravine of Mill Brook, eventually gaining the high, open spread of land beneath hulking Dorset Mountain. The route continuing westward to Pawlet reveals some of the most appealing and capricious topography in the state: bumps, bluffs, nodules and protuberances of the Taconic Mountains are like geologic puns.

Pawlet village poises on the banks of Flower Brook and the Mettawee River. The eclectic cluster of shops and homes complements the singular Taconic landscape. From here Route 30 parallels the Mettawee River through the rich, dark soils of the Mettawee valley, which likely inspired the Indian name, meaning "black earth."

This is good farmland, though limited in acreage. In fact, the bottomland farms of southwest Vermont, bordering New York, are among the best in the state, boasting higher percentage of silage corn acreage than anywhere else in Vermont. Commercial vegetable growing—which is uncommon in the rest of the state—is an important secondary enterprise, subsidiary to dairying.

During Vermont's interim as a separate, independent republic, it coined its own money. Between 1785 and 1788, Reuben Harmon of Rupert minted the republic's copper coins at his mint house in the Mettawee Valley, where a historical marker stands today.

Dozens of abandoned marble quarries pock the town of Dorset, where the earliest quarrying in the state took place in 1785. Smooth walks of the milky-white rock line the main street of Dorset village, a well preserved, quietly wealthy community—long a refuge for writers and artists as well as the rich.

One of the earliest settlers, Cephas Kent, ran a tavern in Dorset which in 1776 hosted the first of a series of conventions that would eventually establish the independent state of Vermont. This first meeting resolved to organize "a free and independent district." The legislature of the Vermont republic later met here many times.

GEORGE WUERTHNER PHOTOS BOTH PAGES

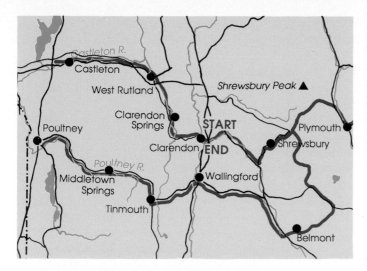

SOUTH OF RUTLAND

The first and second tiers of towns south of Rutland are arguably the most attractive in southern Vermont. In the "Slate Belt," the surrounding knobs of the Taconic Mountains set off the gracious main streets of Castleton, Fairhaven and Poultney. Miles to the east, the birthplace of Calvin Coolidge, 30th president, is a study in the stolid, enduring grace of the Vermont hills and the people that settled them. And in between: high summits, well preserved villages and rivers both vigorous and lazy.

At the northern end of the Taconic Range the mountains turn lumpy. Rocky knolls resemble giant warts; hills that seem classically, smoothly formed break into raw cliff faces, shattering the illusion of rounded perfection. If the Taconics appear to be rather unlikely mountains, they are: they used to lie on the opposite side of the Green Mountains.

The range extends from near Lake Bomoseen to beyond the Massachusetts border. Several major, westward flowing streams, including the Castleton, Poultney, Mettawee, Battenkill and Walloomsac rivers, cut through the range. The

Valley of Vermont defines its eastern boundary and separates it from the Green Mountain Range. Although quite broad at Bennington and Rutland, the Valley of Vermont narrows to a few hundred yards between Danby and North Dorset. The proximity of Vermont's two major ranges belies their geologic dissimilarity, which once puzzled geologists. They are composed of very different rock types and the shales and slates of the Taconics in particular seem incongruous with the rock around them.

Not until scientists linked rocks east of the Green Mountains with the Taconics did the bizarre story begin to unfold. It seems that the Taconics were pushed up and over the Green Mountain Range sometime between 450 and 500 million years ago. These migrating rocks either slid off the western slope of the Green Mountains or actually were pushed to their new location. The sheet of rocks was probably

Above: *Once a popular health spa, the Clarendon Springs Hotel now sits quietly empty.*

Facing page: *The upland town of Tinmouth—too high and rocky to sustain much present-day farming—does best at providing lovely, pastoral scenery.*

JAMES SCHWABEL

continuous at one time; no deep intervening valley separated the two ranges and no streams dissected the Taconics themselves into isolated knobs and peaks. These lowlands today are underlain by marble, an easily eroded rock. (This "marble belt" between the two mountain ranges is evident in the numerous active and inactive quarry holes that dot the Valley of Vermont.) The rocks shoved over from the Green Mountains included layers of marble or limestone, a related rock. They eroded more rapidly than the other displaced rocks, and so became the valleys. Erosion sculpted the more resistant rocks into the Taconic Range.

The Taconics are unusual in another way. Normally, rocks lie atop one another according to the chronological sequence of their formation. The older rocks of the Taconics, however, were thrust atop younger formations, though of course the range itself is a younger geologic feature. If one drilled down through, say, Birdseye Mountain overlooking the Castleton River, eventually he would hit rocks younger than those above.

The village of Clarendon sits squarely in the Valley of Vermont, here drained by the northward-flowing Otter Creek. The first array of Taconic hills is quickly reached by driving west on the road to West Rutland. Tucked in these hills at Clarendon Springs is a rather modest geological phenomenon, which at one time made this hamlet a fashionable resort.

As early as 1776, inhabitants of the area knew of the seep issuing from a crack in the marble river bank. By 1781, some enterprising people had constructed a log cabin for visitors, who came to drink the mineral waters and restored their health. In 1798, a hotel stood by the springs and, by 1835, the grand Clarendon Springs Hotel reigned over the great health mecca. Perhaps it was a clever bit of free advertising, perhaps it was true, but in 1840 the rumor spread that eight families in Clarendon had produced 113 children, 99 of whom attended the same school. Whether this was truth or fiction, the spring water was credited with stimulating this remarkable reproductivity.

In the 19th century, the science of medicine was still in its adolescence; folk cures and remedies dominated. Mineral waters had long been thought to have curative powers, and in the latter half of the 1800s many sought health and restoration at spas and resorts scattered around the country. Train travel enabled the great numbers of middle- and upper-class health seekers to reach their destinations quickly and comfortably. After the railroad arrived in Vermont around 1850, many resorts sprang up, and pre-existing establishments flourished and expanded. Two new hotels were added to the complex at Clarendon Springs after 1850.

The watering places in Vermont and elsewhere provided not only several glasses a day, but also luxurious accommodations and recreational facilities such as bowling alleys, croquet lawns and livery stables. Vacationers were probably just as interested in relaxation and escape from the summer heat of the cities as they were in finding cures to their particular ailments. Modern-day health spas still employ this old-fashioned wisdom.

Unlike most resort hotels in the state, which either burned or were razed long ago, the Clarendon Springs Hotel still stands and has been partially restored in recent years. It is not open to the public but can be viewed from the road.

Marble figured even more dramatically in the social and economic evolution of Rutland and the towns eventually carved from it—West Rutland and Proctor. The "Marble City" grew steadily in the first half of the 19th century, due to nearby marble and slate quarries. When rapid and efficient railroad transportation became possible in 1849, the marble industry boomed, and Rutland tripled in population between 1850 and 1880. For the first and only time in its history, Rutland was the most populous town in the state. Immigrants contributed significantly to Rutland's growth. Attracted by the demand for labor, stonecutters from Italy, Poland, Sweden and Scotland arrived, as did Irish immigrants who built many miles of railroad in Vermont. In 1910, native Italians composed 2.6 percent of Rutland County residents.

In 1886, Proctor and West Rutland split off from the original town of Rutland. The land within these two towns contained rich marble deposits, from which various quarrying companies profited greatly. It was the people involved with marble pushed for the autonomy of these two villages. The Proctor family, in particular, for whom one of the newly created towns was named, was a wealthy and powerful force in Vermont politics for several decades. They controlled the Republic Party and thus wielded great influence over the

EFFIN OLDER

State House, as well as Vermont's congressional delegation. Redfield Proctor—the founder of the Vermont Marble Company and U.S. Senator—was a member of the Senate committee responsible for construction of federal buildings in the nation's capital. Proctor made certain these were built of Vermont marble—from his quarries. The Supreme Court building, for example, wears a facade of Proctor's rock.

While the town of Proctor remains a finishing center for marbles quarried at the Dorset Mountain operation in Danby, and a few active quarries remain at West Rutland, the heyday of quarrying passed in these towns long ago. Where the route described here passes through downtown West Rutland, the frayed-at-the-edges look about the large homes and shop fronts testifies to the former glory of another Vermont town. Route 4A parallels the Castleton River and, on the opposite bank, four-lane Route 4. The gap cut by the river in the

Above: *A serendipitous still life.*

Facing page: *To keep wooden bridges from deteriorating too quickly in the wet New England climate, early bridge builders "covered" them. This one spans the Cold River in North Clarendon.*

JAMES SCHWABEL

Taconic Range is an impressive one, walled by cliffs and precipitous slopes. The outcropping rocks are worth examining, as these cross-sections reveal the rocks that were thrust over the Green Mountains from the east. Purplish, green and mottled slates like those quarried in the region are among those exposed in the road cuts.

Route 4A intersects Route 30 at Castleton Corners. The village of Castleton is celebrated for its Greek Revival buildings, many designed by Thomas Royal Dake, who worked here in the early 19th century. Among others, he is responsible for the Congregational Meeting House, now known as the Federated Church.

Castleton, and the neighboring towns of Fair Haven and Poultney, formed the center of a major slate industry in the late 1800s. The rock was first quarried in Vermont at Fair Haven, in 1839. In 1848, the first slate-roofed barn was built on present-day Route 22A, just south of Fair Haven. It still stands. Such longevity attests to the quality of slate as a roofing material, to which use it once was widely put. Slate has also been used for flagstones, blackboards, school slates, gravestones and, decoratively, in windowsills and mantelpieces.

As with the marble industry, slate quarrying boomed following the advent of the railroad. Having learned their skill in the slate quarries of their homeland, Welsh immigrants found employment and new homes in western Vermont towns, which boasted one of the highest concentrations of Welsh in the United States.

Although not so important as it once was, the slate industry continues to operate in the region. Quarrying companies maintain headquarters in Poultney, Fair Haven and West Pawlet, and another company in Castleton crushes the rock as a replacement for sand and gravel in concrete blocks.

Poultney, like Castleton, possesses a spacious, elegant downtown and central residential district. Horace Greeley, Poultney's most famous citizen, lived in West Haven, but worked as a young man in Poultney setting type and later in the office of the *Northern Spectator* newspaper. Greeley became one of the greatest journalists of his day and founded the *New York Tribune*. During part of his stint as typesetter in Poultney, Greeley boarded at the Eagle Tavern, frequented in even earlier times by Ethan Allen.

PETER LEMON

JAMES SCHWABEL

Route 140 follows the Poultney River upstream to Middletown Springs, site of another former mineral spring resort. The Middletown spa boasted not just one but three separate springs—the waters of which could be mixed, or drunk in a particular sequence, according to the ailment. The Montvert Hotel, which quartered the faithful of Middletown's waters, was built in 1870 and demolished in 1906. Pines now stand on the site.

The route returns to lesser-known byways as it climbs to the ridgetop town of Tinmouth. Little of note has occurred here since revolutionary times, when three soldiers shot a supposed Tory one night, and later discovered that "nothing really unpatriotic could be laid against the man."

Tinmouth's most outstanding attributes are its views: one from Tinmouth Mountain and the other on the road's descent into Wallingford and the Valley of Vermont. The former unfolds at the north end of Tinmouth Mountain, where the road winds through a rock-strewn pass between two higher knobs. At the eastern edge of town, the road climbs again through dense woods, then crests at the top of a long, open hillside. The White Rocks east of Wallingford stand out as obvious light patches on the dark slope of the Green Mountains. In recent years, these quartzite cliffs and ledges have been one of two peregrine falcon hacking and release sites in Vermont.

Above: Middletown Springs Inn.
Left: The "White Rocks" near Wallingford not only are visible from miles away, they also command a superb view. The trail into the Green Mountain National Forest is steep but short, and makes a good day hike.

Facing page: The Poultney River is one of several major streams in southwest Vermont to cut through the Taconic Mountains and join the Hudson River drainage in New York state. All other streams in Vermont are in either the Champlain or the Connecticut River watershed.

GEORGE WUERTHNER

ROBERT C. SIMPSON

The tour route crosses Route 7 at Wallingford, whose most notable former resident, Paul Harris, founded Rotary International—a service club for professional men (and recently, women). Harris' childhood home on Route 7 is designated by a historical marker.

Continuing eastward, Route 140 follows the narrow intervale of the Roaring Brook. It climbs steeply, crossing the Long Trail and then dipping into the tidy mountain hamlet of East Wallingford. At the crossroads, the traveler should take Route 155 south to the turnoff to Belmont. This unacclaimed hamlet surely ranks as one of the most handsome, untarnished examples of the "ideal" early New England community. The

Left: Farm in Shrewsbury.

Facing page, left: Lyman Batcheller built his pitchfork factory in Wallingford in 1848. The forks, hoes, rakes and other farm implements manufactured here were sent around the world.
Right: The black-and-white warbler is common in deciduous woods and feeds primarily on the trunks and larger branches of trees.

village half-embraces circular Star Lake, an irresistibly photogenic scene when viewed from the south shore. Shrewsbury Peak stands silhouetted against the horizon, while closer, more modest prominences fill in the landscape just beyond the lake's far shore. Houses on the west side of the lake are visible but unobtrusive.

More highland scenery lies along the curving road to Healdville and Route 103. The Crowley Cheese Factory looms conspicuously over the road: a dark, three-story barn where cheese has been manufactured since 1882. Visitors are welcome.

The tour route crosses Route 103, and continues on a paved way northwestward to the crossroads community of Hortonville—another tiny settlement in the mountain town of Mount Holly. After several miles of highland woods and questionable intersections, one should arrive in North Shrewsbury, at the foot of Shrewsbury Peak. Seemingly forgotten by the late 20th century, this quiet village features an authentic-looking general store and views of the summits to the north.

The adventuresome traveler will want to make a rather extended side trip to these mountains in the Calvin Coolidge State Forest, and then continue to the birthplace of Calvin Coolidge in Plymouth Notch. An unpaved mountain road connects North Shrewsbury to Route 100, and from it a short but steep hiking trail leads to the top of Shrewsbury Peak. Interested spelunkers should inquire about several caves located south of Woodward Reservoir, along Route 100.

The Coolidge homestead in Plymouth.

The way becomes rather more tame as one heads south on Route 100, a major north-south corridor through the middle of the state. At Plymouth Union, the tour turns east onto Route 100A. After a steep ascent through a rugged ravine, the road levels out in a wide, circular opening in the wooded hills that vaguely resembles an amphitheater. The maintained meadows, the silence of the encompassing mountains, the obvious focal point—a solitary cluster of buildings atop a central hill—all indicate that despite its austerity, this was a place of import, a place of drama.

The Calvin Coolidge birthplace in Plymouth Notch remains one of the most popular historic sites in the Green Mountain State. Yet it undoubtedly belongs in a book on backroads Vermont, for it captures perfectly an a facet of the Vermont character nearly impossible to put into words, yet clear and undeniable in the configuration of houses, barns, fields and woods so carefully preserved here. That ideal combines endurance, self-sufficiency and independence, a bit stubborn and hard-nosed. It is also cherishes simplicity and believes in pragmatism and humility.

Calvin Coolidge, 30th president of the United States, was born on July 4, 1872 in a house in back of the general store his father ran. He spent his boyhood here, and returned frequently throughout the remainder of his life to relax in his Vermont hills. News of President Warren Harding's sudden death came to Vice President Coolidge while he was here on

ROBERT C. SIMPSON

The two-foot-high showy lady's-slipper grows in bogs and swampy woods.

one of his visits. At 2:47 a.m. on August 3, 1923, Coolidge was sworn into office by his own father. President Coolidge is buried in the small cemetery nearby.

The tour resumes at North Shrewsbury, where a short stint of backtracking is required to get onto the road to the village of Shrewsbury. This hilltop community and the surrounding highland woods have attracted noticeable wealth. Old colonial homes and modern boxy mansions are scattered along the rolling dirt road. The village itself commands a fine view to the south.

At Cuttingsville, Route 103 follows the Mill River downstream to the Clarendon Gorge, where the river suddenly is funnelled into a constricted, rock-walled channel. The Long Trail crosses the gorge with a suspension footbridge, only a 75-yard walk down from the trailhead parking lot. A short section of dirt road connects Route 103 to Clarendon on Route 7, where the tour began.

THE CHAMPLAIN LOWLANDS

ROBERT MAUST

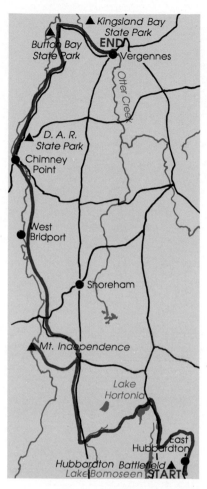

Left: American troops fleeing the outpost at Mount Independence were caught here at Hubbardton by the pursuing British forces, on July 7, 1777. It was the only battle of the Revolutionary War fought in Vermont.

Facing page: Lake Champlain, Shoreham.

HUBBARDTON BATTLEFIELD TO KINGSLAND BAY

Like the first intermittent drops of rain before a heavy summer shower, the peppering of lakes and ponds near Lake Champlain's southern tip foreshadow, it seems, this generous spread of water—the sixth-largest freshwater lake in the United States. Among the more modest, adjacent bodies of water—referred to collectively as the "Lake District"—Lake Bomoseen is the biggest, and also the biggest wholly contained within the Green Mountain State. But even all the pools, ponds and lakes in Vermont lumped together hardly measure up to Champlain, 109 miles long and 11 miles across at its widest.

From the open hilltop where the Battle of Hubbardton took place, the Lake District lies immediately to the west and north. Ridges to the west, silhouetted against the sky, give no hint of the thread of water—the elongated southern terminus of Champlain—that stretches at their base. The Hubbardton Battlefield is an auspicious spot to begin a tour of the Champlain lowlands, not only for the broad views it offers, but also for its prominent place in Revolutionary War history. Hubbardton was the only battle fought on Vermont soil and, while the Americans suffered severe losses in this

51

Right: *The chirp of the spring peeper is a familiar and welcome harbinger of warmer months to come.*
Center: *The Champlain lowland is an ancient lake bottom—thus its flatness and fertility.*

ROBERT C. SIMPSON

KEN LAYMAN; ROBERT MAUST PHOTOGRAPHY

engagement, subsequent events led to the significant British defeat at the Battle of Bennington (which actually took place in present-day New York state).

From Hubbardton to Lake Hortonia, Route 30 skirts the shores of Beebe Pond, Echo Lake and Hortonia itself. Nearby, Half Moon Pond State Park offers the only public camping and picnicking facilities among the dozen or so separate water bodies in the immediate vicinity. Lake Bomoseen State Park to the south is the other exception to this unfortunate rule: public beaches, parks, even fishing access points are rare or nonexistent along the many miles of shoreline in this area. Even on Lake Champlain private ground is predominant, public land occasional. At their worst, lakeshores look like the northern end of Lake Hortonia, which, although a lovely lake in itself, is obscured by densely packed summer "camps." At

best, privately owned lakeshore is undeveloped, backed by farmland or marshes. The undeveloped parcels are gradually, steadily disappearing, however, as farmers and other large-acreage owners in the Champlain Valley (as well as elsewhere in Vermont) bow to financial pressures, selling their land for subdivisions or other, more lucrative development.

More than 300 million years ago, geologists believe, a great block of the earth's crust dropped down between the Adirondack Mountains and the Green Mountains and became the precursor to present-day Lake Champlain and adjacent lowlands. Much later, within the last 3 million years, a series of glaciers—at least four—shrouded Vermont and much of North America in a sheet of continental ice. The last glacial period peaked about 18,000 years ago, and the last glacier left Vermont about 10,000 years ago. That glacier—a

PETER LEMON

Left: A summer "camp" on Lake Champlain.

slow-moving, vast river of ice—gouged deeper into the bedrock of the valley, changing its configuration. After the ice retreated as far north as Burlington about 12,500 years ago, the glacier blocked all drainage to the north and meltwater filled the topographical trough to form a huge freshwater lake. Geologists have dubbed this glacial water body Lake Vermont, and it extended into the foothills of the Green Mountains. The outlet was at its southern end, so that Lake Vermont was part of the Hudson River drainage. Great quantities of lake sediments were deposited.

As the ice receded even farther, the land began to rise, relieved of the great weight of the glacier. But melting ice also raised the sea level, faster than the land rose. Eventually, sea water reached up the St. Lawrence River to Lake Vermont and the freshwater lake became an arm of the vast "Champlain Sea," although with only half the salinity of the ocean. Marine animals inhabited this cold, briny environment, including whales, clams and oysters. Their fossils have been found in the marine sediments that accumulated at that time.

Another, briefer period of cold allowed glacial ice to creep south and again block drainage in the Champlain Valley. The entire cycle repeated itself, but about 10,000 years ago, the glaciers left permanently. The land to the north rose high enough to block out the Atlantic Ocean, but the southern end of the lowland, having shed its ice earlier, rose even higher. The valley tilted northward and the lake drained toward Canada, as it does to this day.

The soils and situation of the Champlain Valley make it the best farmland in Vermont. Its relatively even topo-

While the number of dairy cows and dairy farms in the state has declined, the production of milk has grown. This is largely because farmers have concentrated on areas with better soils and warmer summer temperatures. Bridport, shown here, has one of the highest densities of dairy cows in Vermont.

GEORGE WUERTHNER PHOTOS BOTH PAGES

graphy—although more rolling than flat farther from the lakeshore—and the rich clay soils allow extensive and healthy croplands. Surrounded by mountains, close to the temperature-moderating lake, this region enjoys a longer frost-free season, lower annual precipitation and less extreme temperatures than any other part of the state.

From Orwell to Ferrisburg, this near-shore drive passes through beautiful fields and pasture lands. Large orchards blanket the softly undulating terrain and an ever-present spaciousness is reminiscent of the heartland of America—Kansas, perhaps, or Iowa. The lake, the Adirondacks across its gleaming surface, and the Green Mountains to the east remind one, however, that this is not the Midwest but a pocket of plenty on the nation's eastern . The best time of year to see this part of Vermont is spring, when the acres of

fruit trees turn pink and fragrant; when newly-sprung grass is a tender apple-green, and the graceful urn-shaped elms (those that have escaped Dutch elm disease) along the roadsides resemble giant bouquets of bending ferns.

Mt. Independence in Orwell saw considerable activity during the Revolutionary War. Once considered more strategically important than Fort Ticonderoga—the old fort waits along a poorly-signed road that eventually turns to dirt. Only in 1975, after 200 years of neglect, did the Vermont Division of Historic Preservation open the site to the public. Visitor facilities are minimal. A small notice on the split-rail fence enclosing the grounds informs visitors that this is "...the least disturbed major Revolutionary War site in the U.S." Although existing visitor facilities are restricted to a small parking area and three short hiking trails, the pleasant hilltop views and the pervading sense past turbulentce make Mt. Independence well worth the extra effort it takes to get there.

The rocky knob overlooking the water was the site of fort construction in 1776 when word came that the Declaration of Independence had been signed. The fort was named to commemorate the historic event. Four hundred yards from the fort, a floating bridge stretched across the water to Fort Ticonderoga. Troops from New Jersey, Massachusetts, New York, Connecticut and Vermont were stationed here and at one time Mt. Independence served as headquarters for the Army of the North. Several ships were built here, and later became part of the fleet led by Benedict Arnold at the battle of Valcour Island. This fierce naval battle between British and American forces took place in October of 1776, off present-day South Hero, Vermont. In July of the following year, the British moved down the lake to take Fort Ticonderoga. The Americans retreated across the pontoon bridge but did not destroy it, thus enabling the British to follow with little delay. The rear guard of the retreating American troops was attacked at Hubbardton.

Farther north, the next significant protrusion of land into Champlain is Larrabee's Point. In 1787, John Larrabee bought the hotel which had been built here shortly before the Revolutionary War. He added a store, docks and a ferry. To this day, a ferry runs between New York and Vermont in the summer months, inviting a side-trip to the restored Fort Ticonderoga.

From Larrabee's Point, Route 74 leads into the main village of Shoreham, a town settled in 1766 by Captain Ephraim Doolittle. This revered town father, remembered in a stone marker near the village meeting hall, served as a soldier in the French and Indian Wars under General Amherst and witnessed the British capture of Fort Ticonderoga and Crown Point in 1759. Like many other early pioneers, Doolittle became impressed with Vermont during work on the Crown Point Military Road and returned after his tour of duty to carve a community out of the wilderness.

An unpaved road heads west from the village to the lakeshore, which the road then parallels northward until it meets Route 125. At Leonard's Bay (Lapham Bay on some maps) a public boat access allows visitors a chance to get down to the water without trespassing.

Limestones at D.A.R. State Park.

Another lake access point off Route 125 marks the mouth of Whitney Creek, where a marsh provides habitat for many species of waterfowl and other wetland dwellers. Marshes are a speciality of the lake's east shore. Separate factors combine to produce an abundance of wetland acreage: clay soils hamper drainage; the lowland's gentle gradient

Dead Creek Wildlife Area near Patton.

means that streams are slow and unable to carry sediments, which collect on the lake's edge.

Marshes are among the most biologically rich ecosystems in the world. Vegetation is thick and diverse. Many animal species, from insects and reptiles to birds and mammals, live in or visit the marsh. North of Whitney Creek Marsh, the Dead Creek marshlands, lower Otter Creek and the mouth of Little Otter Creek have been protected as waterfowl or wildlife management areas. Vermont possesses

some of the best marshes left in New England. In the past, wetlands throughout the northeastern U.S. were viewed as "useless," and were drained to become farmland or other developed ground. They became dumping grounds for human garbage or collection points for pollutants entering drainage systems upriver.

Travelers should not assume public access to the Champlain marshlands or other wildlife management areas in the state, even though they are managed by the Vermont Fish

Addison County has become the center of apple production in the state. Shoreham, Orwell and Cornwall are particularly heavy producers.

and Game Department. Some areas are closed to protect nesting birds or other sensitive species at certain times of year. Also, private inholdings or encircling private land may hinder legal access. Prior consultation with the Fish and Game Department is advised (see Resources section at back of book) for those who want to venture farther than a few feet from their car.

The graceful Lake Champlain Bridge arches across narrowing waters between Chimney Point in Vermont and historic Crown Point in New York state. Chimney Point is so named because of the chimneys left standing after the French abandoned settlements there and a fort across the lake at Crown Point after the French and Indian War.

The British, following the French retreat northward along the lake, claimed the site in 1759 though the French had largely demolished the fort and settlements before fleeing. The British leader, Lord Jeffrey Amherst, had his men level what remained of the old fort, and then he embarked on an

GEORGE WUERTHNER

GEORGE WUERTHNER

Left to right:
Ruins of the Crown Point Fort in New York, located across a narrow isthmus from Chimney Point.
Nineteenth-century industry grew up next to ready sources of hydropower. These old mills are on the Otter Creek, in Vergennes.
Yellow lady's-slipper.

ambitious project: the construction of the largest colonial fort ever built on the continent. He also ordered the construction of the Crown Point Military Road, which became so important to the later settlement of Vermont. The road connected Crown Point to Fort Number 4 on the Connecticut River, solidifying Amherst's control over the region. The ruins of Amherst's bastion are preserved at the New York Crown Point State Park, where a fine visitor's center offers exhibits and a slide show, telling the tale of this historic spot and of the Lake Champlain region.

Just north of Chimney Point, D.A.R. State Park features interesting natural as well as human artifacts. Fossils of trilobites, brachiopods and bryozoans in the shoreline limestones

indicate that this piece of ground once lay beneath an ancient ocean, several hundred million years before Champlain became an arm of the sea during glacial times. Good outcrops of shale also bespeak of another long-ago environment during which water deposited fine silts and muds instead of shelled marine animals.

The John Strong Mansion at the state park preserves a much more recent specimen: a 1795 home restored by the Daughters of the American Revolution, furnished with period pieces and featuring collections of china and glass.

The shoreline drive continues north to Button Bay State Park in Ferrisburg, where button-shaped rocks have formed in the heavy clay soils. Limestones here and on tiny

Button Island bear the remains of corals, snails and other prehistoric organisms.

Kingsland Bay State Park offers the fossil aficionado more intriguing limestones and the chance to enjoy a piece of undeveloped public land. There are no visitor facilities yet. Nearby Otter Creek and Little Otter Creek empty into Champlain, providing waterfowl and other wildlife with excellent, marshy habitat. Little Otter Creek, one of the most extensive undisturbed marshes in Vermont, and is best seen and appreciated by boat or canoe.

ROBERT C. SIMPSON

DICK DIETRICH

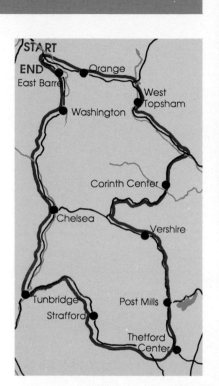

GEORGE WUERTHNER

Left: *Early autumn snows near Chelsea.*

Facing page: *The white clapboard buildings, the broad town commons around which the rest of the village is ordered—this scene in Chelsea captures an ideal image of America that many people seem to find in Vermont.*

THROUGH TUNBRIDGE, THETFORD, CHELSEA

It's a good bet that Orange County is the most-photographed place in Vermont. In any Vermont *Life* magazine photo essay, on any postcard rack, or between the hard covers of any Vermont coffee table book, classic scenes from this pastoral, hill-and-dale country appear reliably and more frequently than images from any other part of the Green Mountain State.

The storybook villages, the softly swelling ground, the tapestry of handkerchief-size fields, wooded hills and thread-like streams—undeniably these are attractive. But Vermont boasts many attractive places, scenes that are grander, more spacious, wilder, or more ostentatiously civilized. Other parts of the state feature higher mountains, wider rivers, broader fields and healthier farms. There are both poorer towns and richer ones than those in Orange County. In fact, Orange can probably claim the one superlative—most photographed, and perhaps another—most beloved piece of Vermont.

When the non-Vermonter thinks of Vermont, he most likely envisions an Orange County kind of scene. Land not flat, yet not rugged either. Villages small, quiet, tidy and well preserved. Modest farms. In all, a place that is human-scale, comfortable and comprehensible because it is not large, nor complex, nor ambitious. The jaded, late-20th-century urban American immediately recognizes Orange County as a spiritual refuge, a replenishing spring of hope in the human enterprise, for a society that collectively has moved so far from its

In Orange County, the vegetation begins to take on a more "northern" look, as trees such as red spruce and aspen—typical of the boreal forest—begin to dominate.

GEORGE WUERTHNER

connection to natural and personal communities that it has nearly forgotten its thirst for these values.

From the hillside village of East Barre, Route 110 leaves Highway 302 for the town of Washington on a ridgetop path that eventually leads to the watershed divide between the Winooski and White rivers. The First Branch of the White flows through the shiretown of Chelsea, where an elegant and broad green spreads before the county courthouse and the Chelsea meeting house. Corn fields like banners spread along the river, covering the narrow terraces between stream and hillside.

Tunbridge is a peaceful community of some 400 people for 361 days of the year. For four days, however, it is a rowdy, bustling city of 20,000 people who come here every September for the Little World's Fair—a tradition since 1867. The fair includes livestock exhibits, fiddler contests, horse pulls, displays of everything from flowers to old artifacts, and dancing.

The towns of Washington, Chelsea and Tunbridge, despite their charm, have a look of benign neglect. Churches and clapboard homes have not seen a fresh coat of paint for too many years; here and there a mobile home huddles in the trees or a dilapidated cabin hugs the roadside. Beyond the hill

PETER LEMON PHOTOS

between Tunbridge and Strafford, however, the apperence of the towns and their inhabitants quickly changes.

The regal, two-story 1799 Strafford Town Hall gleams with clean, new white paint. Carefully preserved buildings encircle a small green, among which stand a bicycle shop, of all things, in this tiny Vermont village. The farms feature clear ponds and stables, no junked tractors or lean and dirty horses. Strafford sits within commuting distance of both Dartmouth College in Hanover, New Hampshire and the Vermont Law School in South Royalton, which both have brought money without heavy commercialization to these upper Connecticut River valley towns.

The pink Gothic Revival mansion of Justin Smith Morrill stands out among the other modestly white homes of Strafford. This 17-room house was to have been the retirement home of the U.S. Senator, who served in Congress from 1855 to 1898 (as a senator from 1867). Although Morrill never spent much time here because of his political duties, he did do significant work in Washington. His greatest contribution to the country and future generations was the Land Grant College Act, which established the present system of land-grant colleges in this country. Morrill was also largely responsible for the passage of the protective tariff act of 1861 which made it possible for U.S. copper (Strafford was a major producer at the time) to compete with imports, mostly from Great Britain. Morrill was a major booster of establishing the Library of Congress and building the Washington Monument. His home, now maintained by the Vermont Division of Historic Preservation, is open to the public.

South Strafford seesm similarly well-to-do, in an understated way, as do the villages of the neighboring town to the east, Thetford. The red-brick Methodist Church peeks above

Above: The Ompompanoosuc eventually flows into the Connecticut River.
Left: The austere but elegant Strafford Town Hall.

PETER LEMON

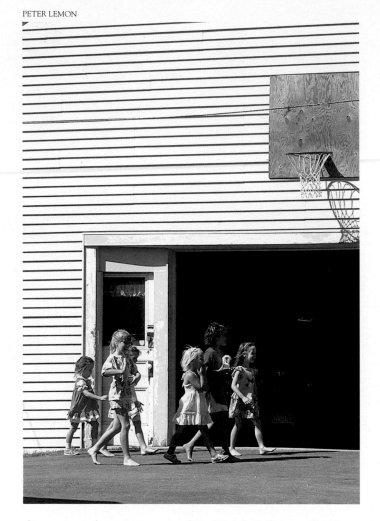

the trees on the pretty approach to Thetford Center. Post Mills is surprisingly sophisticated, too, after one passes the gargantuan gray shell of the old mill.

Route 113 parallels the Ompompanoosuc River through West Fairlee—remarkably poorer than the previous two towns—and Vershire, the least populated town in the county. Now a hilltop backwater in the center of Orange County, Vershire was once a booming copper mining town—along with Strafford and the town of Corinth to the north—and employed some 2,000 people during peak production. In 1880, it recorded the second-highest population in the county.

Copperas, or iron pyrite, indicates the possible presence of copper. Copperas mined in Strafford led to the discovery of copper there in 1793. It is claimed that before production of copper began in the Lake Superior region in the 1840s, the three Orange County towns accounted for three fifths of all copper produced in the U.S.

Whether or not Orange County was the nation's biggest producer in the first half of the 19th century, the deposits proved most productive after 1870. In 1880, Vermont produced about 5.5 million pounds of copper, compared with more than 20 million pounds in the Lake Superior mines, and 7 million pounds from deposits in Butte, Montana.

The Vermont Copper Mining Company, under the leadership of entrepreneur Smith Ely of New York City, made Vershire the state's leading copper town. Many miners were natives of Cornwall and Ireland. Finns came to the Vermont copper mines from granite quarries in Quincy, Massachusetts. The mines prospered under the direction of Ely and with the advent of the railroad. Ore traveled the tracks to Boston, Connecticut and Baltimore where smelters concentrated the ore. The rails never actually reached Vershire, though Ely made many tries at getting a spur built to his mines. Eventually, he made do with a highway that linked the Ely Mines to the railroad.

By 1868, the Vermont Copper Mining Company opened its own smelting operation. Initially requiring huge quantities of wood to fire the furnaces, the copperas and copper operations resulted in an unwanted byproduct: acid rain. The sulfuric acid that fell onto the forests and into the streams of this area make today's acid rain seem insignificant by comparison. The most acidic soils now support birch trees, tolerant of acid conditions, but few other tree species inhabit the old smelting area. To this day, trout cannot survive in the acid waters of the Ompompanoosuc between West Fairlee and Thetford, and on its West Branch below South Strafford.

Only two years after the peak of Vermont production, the mines in 1882 had declined in profitability. Copper prices fell; deepening mine shafts cost more to maintain; in addition, miners extracted lower-quality ore. To add to the company's problems, Ely's popularity waned after he tried to have the town of Vershire renamed for himself. Ely's grandson took up residence in the town, which no other family member ever

DICK DIETRICH

Some people claim that what keeps Orange County so purely "Vermontish" is perennial economic depression and the concomitant lack of development and opportunity for the residents. Waits River.

did, and became paymaster. Unfortunately, he flaunted his wealth, superior education and social class, increasing the workers' resentment of their employers.

In 1883, the grandson's poor management practices combined with falling copper prices to produce a financial crisis in the company. Ely ordered the workers, who already were owed back pay, to halt operations. The "Ely War" began as angry miners and smeltermen raided the company store and then surrounded the grandson's mansion. He escaped to Rhode Island while the Vermont National Guard moved in and arrested the ringleaders.

Ely sold his mining company the next year and, by 1905, it failed completely after the new owner struggled in vain to make a go of it. The Strafford mines saw flurries of activity during the two World Wars, but since then Orange County's copper deposits—and there *is* still ore in the ground—have been undisturbed.

From the main village in Vershire, the route continues on Highway 113 to the intersection with the road to Corinth Corners. The views of hills, meadows, farms and tiny but delightful hamlets of Corinth make this upland town a favorite among photographers.

At Goose Green, the route turns left, then soon after, right, remaining paved all the way to Route 25 near East Corinth. The uplands feature spruce and birch woods, boggy spots and occasional raw clearings where recent logging operations have taken place.

The Waits River flows to the Connecticut from the heights of Orange and Topsham towns. Once again, settlements here have the worn, rather weary look of places long since bypassed by modern events. The town of Orange remains largely a farming town, but its population peaked more than a century and a half ago, in 1830, when 1,000 people and 5,000 sheep crowded the hills and valley bottoms.

GEORGE WUERTHNER

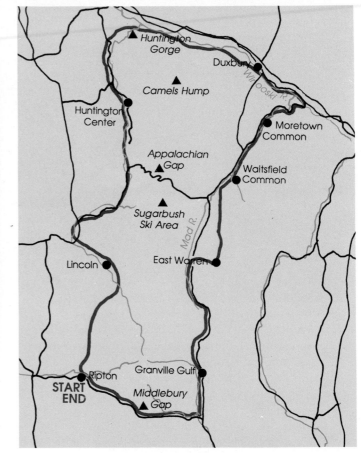

THROUGH RIPTON, HUNTINGTON, WARREN

Some of the highest peaks, most dazzling waterfalls and gorges and finest ski areas in Vermont occupy the narrow crest of the Green Mountains between Middlebury Gap and the valley of the Winooski River. The natural beauty of this area has attracted wealth. Out-of-state second-home buyers

GEORGE WUERTHNER

JANIS MIGLAVS

and resort developers favor the Mad River valley in particular. Starkly modern, angular structures appear suddenly around a bend in a potholed dirt road. Elaborately carved wooden signs, gilded with gold, stand at entrances to "exclusive communities" and luxury-home developments. But beyond these obvious demonstrations of affluence, meticulously preserved villages and tidy, freshly painted farmhouses and country estates testify to the concern and, more significantly, the wealth of the property owners and the municipalities that benefit from hefty property taxes.

The contrast between richer and poorer towns along this tour demonstrates that, while money has changed the look of the state, it clearly also takes money to keep Vermont looking like "Vermont." The ironic juxtaposition of extreme affluence and dire poverty, even within the same towns, is particularly evident in this rocky, mountainous area where the land itself has never been generous and the influx of out-of-state money has driven up living costs even more.

The most desperate, squalid-looking habitations on any tours featured in this book line the road north of Ripton, where this trip begins. While the village itself is charming, the scattered shacks and trailers to the north—between Ripton and South Lincoln—are not merely ramshackle. They look bombed-out. And yet, between decaying trailers and yards heaped with wrecked cars, newer homes alternate with well maintained farmhouses. The poverty is not ubiquitous even in the state's poorest town, which is Ripton.

At South Lincoln, the striking profile of Mount Abraham comes into view. And the bedrock-gouging New Haven River plunges from the heights of the Green Mountains, carving boulder-filled gorges. The rock ribs of the mountains seem to poke out everywhere in this region: the Bristol Cliffs Wil-

Above: *Along some backroads are left the cars that used to drive them.*
Left: *Despite statistics that place Ripton— in terms of wealth—near the bottom of all Vermont towns, most of it looks like any other pleasant, quiet village in the state.*

Facing page: *Texas Falls in the Green Mountain National Forest.*

67

Huntington Center. PETER LEMON

derness sits south and west of the road to Rocky Dale on Route 17. At the road junction, an impressive escarpment rises above the trees immediately to the north and, to the right of the road, sharply angular, blocky bedrock is exposed.

Route 17 continues to the town of Starksboro, where open upland fields offer sweeping views of the mountain crest. On the other side of the Green Mountain ridge, ski areas have helped make the Mad River valley popular and well-to-do. On the west side, however, farms and the villages have that time-worn, weary look. Huntington Center, for example, in the shadow of Camel's Hump—Vermont's fourth-highest mountain at 4,083'—enjoys a spectacular location but not the revival of its eastern neighbors. Farther down the road, tract houses dot the valley of the Huntington River. It's a good bet that many of these belong to Burlington commuters. Interstate 89 is only a few miles to the north.

The Green Mountain Audubon Center in Huntington features interpretive classes and trails winding through its 230 acres of woods and wetland. While the center is open year-round, a phone call to check ahead is recommended. The nature center is strategically located near two outstanding natural areas—the Huntington Gorge and Camel's Hump. The former, mainly a geological attraction, boasts a narrow rock-walled chasm with deep potholes carved out of the greenish stone. In warmer months, this gorge becomes a popular swimming hole (note that it is privately owned).

Camel's Hump is one of only two mountains in the state with a significant zone of alpine tundra near its summit. About 10 acres of alpine tundra, as well as high mountain bogs, enrich this most interesting of Vermont peaks. Here, re-

GEORGE WUERTHNER   PETER LEMON

searchers first documented acid rain damage to the state's high-elevation forests. Since 1965, they discovered, 50 percent the red spruce on Camel's Hump has died due to exposure to acidic precipitation and heavy metals, carried through the atmosphere primarily from Midwestern industrial areas.

A secondary road parallels the Winooski River on its south bank through the towns of Bolton and Duxbury. The Winooski cuts straight through the Green Mountains, and is a superb example of a superimposed stream. Even before the uplift of the Green Mountains, the precursor of today's Winooski flowed from east to west. As the mountains rose, the river sawed through, essentially maintaining its original course. Other superimposed rivers in Vermont are the Lamoille to the north, and the Batten Kill, which slices at right angles through the Taconic Range.

The tangle of roads around Waterbury, along the Winooski, is potentially confusing. Traveler should be mainly concerned with getting to Moretown Common, the next feature of this backroads tour. The Commons Road, as this upland byway is called locally, parallels the main highway in the Mad River valley. Halfway up the slopes of the Northfield Mountains, it allows some of the best views of Camel's Hump from any direction and, farther south, around Waitsfield Common and East Warren, the ski areas on the east slope of the Green Mountains are plainly visible. The Commons Road leads all the way to East Warren, with only one brief dip back down to Route 100B at Moretown.

The Joslin Round Barn in Waitsfield is a particular feature of this stretch of road. Round barns are uncommon in Vermont—only about a dozen survive. The design apparently originated with the Shakers in Massachusetts, who built a

Above: *Appalachian Gap, between Lincoln Gap to the south and Camels Hump and the Winooski River to the north. Some consider this the most beautiful and interesting stretch of the ridgetop Long Trail.*
Left: *The Mad River churns through a steep, rocky gorge of greenish Camels Hump schist, south of Warren.*

Above: This "general store" in Warren has adapted to serve a more sophisticated clientele.
Right: The Round Barn Inn, near Warren.

round stone barn there in 1824. All the round barns in Vermont were built between 1899 and World War I.

Just beyond the crossroads at East Warren, the main paved highway turns west for Warren village and Route 100. Despite extensive development in the Mad River valley in the last two decades, the village of Warren itself has stayed small, and it maintains a tasteful Old New England air that other rapid-growth communities have lost. And yet the "yuppie" flavor, too, is undeniable here and throughout the valley. The area's transformation from just another sleepy, Vermont farm valley to the pastoral refuge of urbanites and the affluent began in the early 1960s with the growth of trailside and bot-

tom-of-the-lift homes and vacation houses at Sugarbush ski area. Within a few years, the well educated, relatively young people who were attracted to the Mad River area were building not only solar-heated homes and prototype "cluster" housing developments; they also were installing an art center, a sports center, shopping centers with specialty shops, an airport, inns and sophisticated restaurants.

Within 20 years, the population of the Mad River valley doubled. Even more significant demographic shifts occurred in the ratio of vacation to permanent residences, in the inflation of land values and in the amount of commercial activity. In 1968, there were 568 vacation homes in the towns of War-

The Joslin Round Barn near Warren is one of only about a dozen round barns left in the state.

ren, Waitsfield and Fayston; by 1973 there were 895. Warren's grand list swelled from $6 million in 1960 to more than $451 million in 1976. Mushrooming commerce in the valley sent the number of retail stores from 14 in 1957 to 49 in 1976.

Although not a "backroad," the drive between Warren and Hancock on Route 100 deserves to be included in any tour of Vermont's great scenery. The route follows the Granville Gulf, a shady defile between the main ridge of the Green Mountains and a subsidiary range known as the Braintree Mountains. At the height of land the streams divide into

Vermont's two major drainages: the waters of the Mad River flow ultimately into Lake Champlain, and the streams that flow south from Granville Gulf join the White River, which then flows into the Connecticut. Abundant water makes this narrow passage a tunnel of greenery and leaf-diffused light. Numerous waterfalls tumble off steep rock walls, including 100' Moss Glen Falls—one of the highest in the state. On the east side of the road a small wooded stand of six acres, within the Granville Gulf Reservation, that is virgin—or nearly so— red spruce and hemlock.

The Sugarbush downhill ski area is one of three in the Mad River Valley. (There are three nordic ski centers as well.) Sugarbush was the first New England ski area to be planned as a destination resort when it opened in 1958, and featured a complete bottom-of-the-lift "ski village."

Route 125 heads west from the crossroads at Hancock, back toward Middlebury Gap and Ripton. Along the way, lovely Texas Falls, just off the main highway, features a narrow flume and water-smoothed potholes. The Long Trail crosses the road at the gap, which like Smuggler's Notch and other high passes in the Green Mountain Range, was carved by streams and glacial ice. The small Middlebury College Snow Bowl ski area is tucked in a steep basin just over the crest.

Middlebury College also owns and operates the Bread Loaf School of English, which hosts a writers conference each summer. The spacious campus spreads gracefully against the backdrop of Bread Loaf Mountain, which originally inspired the name of this former inn and estate of Joseph Battell. A local civic leader, businessman and large landowner. Battell willed thousands of acres of mountain land, as well as the Bread Loaf Inn, to Middlebury College. Battell was also an early advocate of establishing a national forest in Vermont.

The annual writers conference was begun by the poet Robert Frost, who kept a country retreat in Ripton, just west of the Bread Loaf School. This four-time Pulitzer Prize winner bought the house in the 1940s as a place to escape between stints as university instructor and lecturer at various institutions. Before obtaining the Ripton home, Frost for a short time owned a place in Shaftsbury, in southern Vermont. The Shaftsbury farmhouse is privately owned, but Middlebury College bought the Ripton property in 1966, three years after Frost's death and preserves it as a memorial to the man who became Vermont's most famous writer and unofficial poet laureate to the nation.

Moss Glen Falls in grotto-like Granville Gulf.

GEORGE WUERTHNER PHOTOS BOTH PAGES

NORTHERN SHORES AND ISLES

GEORGE WUERTHNER

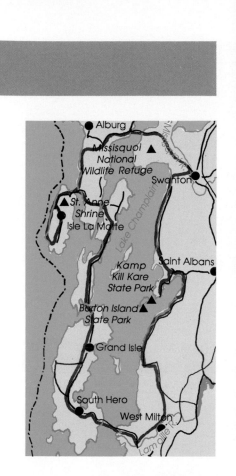

GEORGE WUERTHNER

Left: *Lake Champlain has become a haven for windsurfers. On a day with the right conditions, the beach and waters surrounding Sand Bar State Park are a colorful patchwork of bright sails.*

Facing page: *On South Hero Island, Lake Champlain, in the area more agricultural than any other in Vermont.*

St. Albans Bay Area and Champlain Islands

The Bear Trap Road turns off Route 2 a few hundred yards west of the Lamoille River. Moss-draped rock walls flank the unpaved road for about a mile, then give way to farms and rocky fields. New subdivisions sprout amidst stands of pine or at the edge of cornfields—tendrils of suburbia have begun to entwine the hinterlands of Milton town. The proliferation of access roads and driveways in this area can be confusing; occasionally a stretch of pavement or gravel appears that is not accounted for on maps. There's no need for panic, however, if travelers get "temporarily disoriented." A northward course should eventually lead to the paved Lake Road.

The route continues west and north on Lake Road to the town of Georgia. Along Lake Champlain, Georgia's residences consist mostly of boxy cottages balanced on the extreme edge of the land. This stretch of the tour is discouraging, although the lake views are pleasant. The scarcity of public lake access thwarts visitors' natural desire to stop and savor the vistas of beach, shimmering water and offshore islands.

Fortunately, a few prime locations have been reserved for public use. The St. Albans Bay State Park is a pleasant place to picnic, as is Kamp Kill Kare State Park at the end of St. Albans Point. Kill Kare, once a fashionable summer hotel, later was a boy's camp for many years. Today the restored 1850 structure houses a snack bar and staff apartments. From the boat launch site, one may cruise to Burton Island State

75

Right: *St. Albans village square.*
Far right: *While many Vermont farmers slowly are surrendering their livelihoods in the face of escalating land values and more competitive, productive farms elsewhere, those farms situated on the fertile ground around Lake Champlain still are relatively well off.*

PETER LEMON PHOTOS BOTH PAGES

Park, a short distance offshore. The park also provides a ferry service to those without their own boats. Recently-acquired Woods Island State Park, off the west shore of the Point, is maintained mostly as a natural area, without elaborate visitor facilities.

St. Albans itself, once an important railroad center, for a long time boasted the largest railroad depot in New England. In the late 19th and early 20th centuries, it also was the capital of a dairy empire: the world's largest creamery stood here, and it alone produced 2 million pounds of butter a year (five percent of the total state production) when Vermont was the nation's leading dairy producer.

Close to the Canadian border, St. Albans has seen more than its share of international incidents. From 1807 to 1814, the town was headquarters of a large smuggling operation—the product of President Jefferson's embargo against trade with foreign nations (altered in 1809 to cover only France and Britain and their colonies). Northern Vermonters were particularly hurt by this political maneuver; they had enjoyed a lively trade of beef, furs and lumber prior to the presidential

Above: *Maquam Bay.*
Left: *Kamp Kill Kare State Park.*

ban. Smuggling continued through the War of 1812, during which Vermont cattle herded across the border fed the British Army.

St. Albans also saw the northernmost "engagement" of the Civil War. On October 19, 1864, 22 armed Confederate soldiers held up three banks, stole horses and escaped to Canada with $201,000. One raider wounded in the melee eventually died, and the Confederates shot and killed a visitor to the town The surviving soldiers were eventually captured in Montreal, but Canadian officials claimed the incident had been a legitimate act of war and never extradited them.

Despite its colorful history, St. Albans experienced a long slump following the decline of the railroad industry. Today it shows signs of revitalization—which seem inevitable considering its choice location on the shores of Champlain and its proximity to large population concentrations in Burlington and Montreal.

Highway 36 takes the lakeside route between St. Albans and Swanton. More cabins teeter on the water's brink, and more views span the water to Butler Island and North Hero. At Maquam Bay the road swerves east to the Missisquoi River and the village of Swanton. Some of the oldest traces of human habitation in Vermont have been found in this town.

The first Vermonters lived here between 12,000 and 9,500 years ago, during the waning days of the last glacial period. At that time, Vermont probably resembled the tundra of the Arctic, and was inhabited by herds of caribou and mammoth. Seals, whales and walruses swam the chilly waters of the Champlain Sea. The Paleo-Indians hunted these animals with stone spearheads and knives, about the only artifacts they left to later archaeologists.

As the climate gradually warmed, flora and fauna responded and many of the large mammals the Paleo-Indians depended upon disappeared. From a nomadic hunting society, Indian peoples evolved a hunting-and-gathering culture in which wild plant foods became an important component of diet. About 3,000 years ago, agriculture reached Vermont from Indian groups to the south and west, and a more complex and settled society developed.

The Abnaki tribe lived in western Vermont and gave it many legends and place-names. They lost control of their lands in the Missisquoi area to the powerful Allen family in the late 18th century and subsequently became a nearly forgotten community. They persisted, however, and in the 1970s the estimated 2,000 Abnakis of Vermont began to assert their presence and influence. Today the Indian community is ac-

PETER LEMON

Above: *The Mississquoi River forms a broad delta where it empties into Lake Champlain. Most of the national wildlife refuge is accessible only by boat or canoe.*
Right: *Great blue heron.*

ROBERT C. SIMPSON

tive in providing for the care and betterment of its members, as well as maintaining and cultivating their ethnic identity.

Continuing on the tour route, Highway 78 follows the slow-moving Missisquoi as it creeps toward its rendezvous with Lake Champlain. The Missisquoi National Wildlife Refuge protects the excellent waterfowl and wildlife habitat of the river's broad delta. The stream splits into several channels, isolating damp islands of brush and timberland and creating extensive marshes. (The name, Missisquoi, comes from an Indian word meaning an area of "much waterfowl" and "much grass.") The refuge provides nesting habitat for black ducks, mallards, wood ducks, common goldeneyes, blue-winged teals and hooded mergansers. Other warm-season residents are the great blue heron, American bittern, common gallinule and many songbirds. Perhaps even more significantly, the refuge serves as way station to thousands of migrat-

ing waterfowl that pass through the region every spring and fall. Most ducks that migrate through this section of the Atlantic Flyway come from Quebec and Ontario, the St. Lawrence River Valley and the Hudson Bay area.

Mammals including deer, red fox, beaver, muskrat, red and gray squirrel, raccoon and occasional mink and otter live here, as do a number of warm-water fish species. A nature trail through a portion of the refuge features interpretive signs.

The Champlain "Islands"—the three islands and part of the Alburg Peninsula that make up Grand Isle County—are

78

in one respect obviously distinct from the rest of the state: they are surrounded and dominated by water. Nowhere else in landlocked Vermont is a body of water such an important geographic feature.

Yet, in many other ways, the Islands remain more "Vermont-y" than any other place. Despite proliferation of second homes (a large percentage of them owned by Vermonters), Grand Isle County still retains its strongly rural and still heavily agricultural roots. In fact, it is arguably the most agriculturally-oriented county in the state. In absolute terms, it has fewer cows than any other county with the possible exception of Essex in the northeast. Yet within its small area, a very high density of cows ranked below only Franklin County in 1982. In addition, Isle La Motte and South Hero have important apple-producing areas.

The Islands have escaped commercialization and glamorization, despite the area's obvious value for the tourism and recreation. And, although less visible, the lengthy history of this region—dating back further than in any other part of the state—adds to the sense that here is a prototypical "Vermont" place.

During his general exploration of the St. Lawrence River and its tributaries, the French explorer Samuel de Champlain followed the Richelieu River to its source and, in the year 1609, found the lake on which he bestowed his own name. In 1666, the French established what is now the oldest settlement in the state, at the north end of Isle La Motte. Fort St. Anne housed some 300 men were as a defence against the Mohawk Indians. (The French and their Indian allies, the Algonquins, launched an expedition against the Mohawks late

Above: *The glacial lake soils of the Champlain lowlands, including Grand Isle County, are notable for their dearth of stones. Until the advent of barbed wire in the 1870s, farmers commonly used split rail or stump fences.*
Left: *Samuel de Champlain and his Algonquin Indian guides are commemorated at Fort St. Anne.*

PETER LEMON PHOTOS

Above: *The restored 1783 Hyde Log Cabin.*
Right: *Alburg.*

in 1666.) Within eight years of its construction, however, the French abandoned the fort.

The site is now a religiou as well as a historic site. The St. Anne Shrine, an open-air church, conducts masses daily in summer. A grove of pines and the blue, glimmering surface of the lake compose a peaceful backdrop to the scene. A massive statue of the explorer Champlain and an Indian guide also stands here, overlooking the water. The piece, carved from a single, enormous block of Barre granite, was shown at the 1967 Montreal Expo.

An abandoned quarry at the southern end of Isle La Motte once yielded black "marble" famous for its dark color and the abundance of small fossils visible in its polished surface. Builders used the rock (actually a limestone, not a marble) to construct the stone buildings that are a trademark of this area; they also exported the rock via the lake and ca-

nals at either end, which, after 1835, more closely linked the Champlain region with both southern and northern markets.

The prevalence of limestone bedrock in this region has produced another striking pattern characteristic of Grand Isle County, this one vegetative. The incidence of northern white cedar corresponds almost exactly with a calcitic (limestone) substrate, so that these lacy, elegant trees dominate the Islands, particularly where there is no covering of non-limestone, glacial till. Northern white cedar also graces many miles of shoreline on the mainland.

The tour route returns to the southern tip of the Alburg peninsula and joins Route 2 at its eastern shore. On the island of North Hero, a short side trip to North Hero State Park offers camping on the island's northern tip, beaches, woods and views across the water to the northern Vermont mainland. South toward Carry Bay, a thin isthmus called the

GEORGE WUERTHNER

Isle La Motte's limestone quarries supplied building materials for many older homes in the region.

"Carrying Place" connects the north and south sections of North Hero.

From Knight Point State Park, a day-use park at the southern promontory of North Hero, to the crossing at South Hero, especially fine views reward the southbound traveler: the high peaks of the Green Mountains to the east, including Mt. Mansfield and Camel's Hump; to the west the even higher Adirondacks, with Whiteface Mountain the most prominent summit.

The Hyde Log Cabin in Grand Isle town is one of the oldest extant log cabins in the U.S. Jedidiah Hyde built the homestead in 1783 and cleared the land for livestock and cultivation. One of the first buildings erected in the area, the home—unlike its contemporaries—lasted through several generations of the Hyde family. The cabin was restored in 1956 with as much of the original structure retained as possible. Today the Hyde Log Cabin is furnished with appropriate 18th-century artifacts—furniture, tools, utensils, toys, craftwork.

At South Hero, the route bends east toward the mainland. Across the causeway, Sand Bar State Park is located on the delta at the mouth of the Lamoille River. The adjacent Sand Bar Waterfowl Management Area offers good bird-watching, but many people find windsurfer-watching even more entertaining. The colorful sails decorate this stretch of water in the warmer months of the year, and the beach at the state park is a popular launch site.

DICK DIETRICH

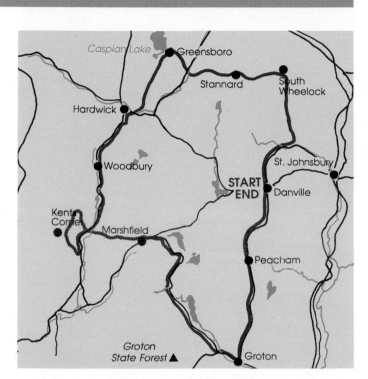

THROUGH THE COUNTIES OF CALEDONIA AND WASHINGTON

This backroads tour is for summer or early autumn. Lengthy unpaved stretches of the route are not terribly appealing in wetter seasons. Also, the abundance of open water to be seen—even if one never ventures from the car—is most attractive and refreshing when the air is contrastingly, almost uncomfortably, warm.

Danville, 10 miles west of St. Johnsbury, combines relatively high elevation with its expansive views of the surrounding piedmont country and the majestic White Mountain Range of New Hampshire to produce one of the better Vermont villages in which to while away a muggy August afternoon.

Perhaps the "quenching" view and atmosphere of Danville led the American Society of Dowsers to locate their national headquarters here. Dowsing, an arcane pursuit that borders on religion for some practitioners, involves locating underground water stores with forked sticks or other devices. The dowser holds the stick horizontally before himself with both hands, and walks over the ground until the stick supposedly points down of its own accord. Dowsers' relative success in predicting good well-drilling sites in this part of the country is easily linked, according to skeptics, to the fact that underground water exists almost everywhere in the water-rich Northeast.

This wealth of water is displayed in particularly charming style in Peacham, south of Danville, and other towns along this tour. Between Danville and Groton, the road itself

Above: Lily pond, Woodbury.

Facing page: Groton.

83

Above: *Caledonia and northern Washington counties are characterized not only by their profusion of ponds, but also by relatively high, rolling terrain. Near Marshfield.*
Right: *The carnivorous pitcher plant.*

favors more White Mountain vistas and tidy upland communities, although wetlands and ponds in abundance are not far from the highway. Carbon-14 dating shows that Stoddard Swamp, a cedar bog with rich and diverse flora just north of the hamlet of Ewell's Mills, is more than 11,000 years old.

Many older bogs in Vermont began as glacially formed depressions called "kettles." When glaciers deposited huge loads of sediment across the land, they often left giant chunks of ice embedded in the unsorted till. The ice eventually melted, leaving a hole. Glacial till often hinders drainage, so the kettles filled with water and bog formation began. Because of environmental conditions in a bog—cold water with a high acid concentration and low oxygen content—biologic activity slows greatly. Skinny cedars or tamaracks at a bog may be decades old, whereas same-size trees on "normal" land may be only 10 to 12 years in age.

Bogs are home to certain plants seen in no other ecological system. Carnivorous plants like the pitcher plant, bladderwort and sundew adapt to the nutrient-deficient bog habitat by capturing and "digesting" insects. Mosses, sedges and shrubs of the heath family tolerate the wet, acid conditions, as do beautiful orchids such as the white bog orchid, yellow lady's-slipper and rose pogonia. Some 30 species of orchids grow in Vermont's bogs and swampy woods.

Peacham Bog in Groton State Park can be reached by some challenging, wet walking north of Lake Groton, but explorers should equip themselves with directions from park personnel, along with compasses.

To reach the south entrance to the large tract of wild woods and ponds in Groton State Park and Forest, this tour route passes through the village of Groton, birthplace of William Scott, the famed "Sleeping Sentinel" of the Civil War. As a young soldier, Scott fell asleep at his post at a Union camp on the Potomac River, was court marshalled and sentenced to execution. Upon hearing of her son's sentence, Scott's mother traveled to Washington to plead with President Lincoln to spare her son's life. Deeply moved, Lincoln pardoned the man, and paid a personal visit to the execution site to make sure that his order was promptly delivered. The president was severely criticized for his compassion; Scott later died in action.

Peacham, looking east to the White Mountains.

DICK DIETRICH

The road through the state forest stays mostly in boulder-thick woods, offering occasional glimpses of Ricker Pond, then Lake Groton to the east. The rocks sprouting gardens of moss and ferns are glacial erratics, plucked by flowing ice from mountain tops or valley walls, then carried and dumped farther "downstream" so to speak. Undoubtedly, glaciers harvested many of these boulders from the jagged cliffs of Owl's Head and the Spice Mountains, between which the road passes north of Lake Groton.

Lake Groton itself offers fine views of these unusual looking peaks, as well as camping and beach facilities. Kettle Pond, a short distance farther along the road, is a botanist's playground with thick growths of snowberry, wintergreen, bunchberry, ferns and blueberries along the shore—as well as striped maple, hobblebush, laurel, labrador tea and turtlehead.

Route 232 intersects the main east-west Highway 2 just a mile east of Marshfield village. The slim stream of the Winooski, which originates in the hills to the north in the town of Cabot, runs through the center of the settlement. From here, the road to East Calais climbs out of the river valley onto high hills, mostly wooded. As the road dives into the river-cut valley of the Kingsbury Branch of the Winooski, it

DICK DIETRICH

PETER LEMON

splits around a large white church seemingly built right in the middle of the roadway. The route to Kents Tavern Museum continues just a few hundred feet to the north off Route 14.

Up again steeply, and down the same way. The dips and swells of the Vermont piedmont can sometimes seem relentless to travelers taking the backroads instead of highways along main water routes. Following the miniature and faded signs to the museum, the road passes the venerable Calais Town Hall, then climbs to the ridgetop cluster of buildings called Kents Corner. The Kent Tavern Museum, a stagecoach stop dating from 1817, is appropriately furnished in Vermont rural style with craft pieces, tools, looms and spinning wheels and period furniture.

The Old West Church stands less than a mile to the south of the intersection at Kents Corner. Recent preservation efforts have maintained the original character of the 1823 building. The church served as a meetinghouse for various religious sects during its long history, including the fanatical Millerites, who believed the world would end in October 1843.

To reach North Calais, travelers either can make a scenic loop through Maple Corner and past Curtis Pond, or retrace the route past the Town Hall and continue north. The village of North Calais perches pleasingly on a cascading mill stream flowing out of Mirror Lake. Northward, the town of Woodbury holds the highest concentration of ponds and lakes of any single town in Vermont. At least 23 bodies of water

DICK DIETRICH

Left: *The Kent Tavern Museum, Calais.*

Facing page, left: *This general-store owner in Groton apparently is not interested in keeping up with the latest trends in window display.*
Right: *Marshfield.*

crowd inside Woodbury's borders, which hosts few people and even less economic wealth.

Early in this century, some 14 granite quarries made Woodbury and adjoining Hardwick one of Vermont's major producing areas. The granite was carried by rail to finishing mills in Hardwick, then shipped to ports all over the world. The industry brought hundreds of laborers to Hardwick, many of them skilled European stonecutters. Hardwick flourished for about two decades, during which time it was nicknamed "Little Chicago" and supported three creameries, two large hotels, many shops, a broom factory, several saloons and five churches. In recent decades, however, Hardwick has suffered continual emigration and more than 15 percent of its inhabitants now live below the poverty level (the state average is approximately nine percent).

Crossing the Lamoille River, the route heads toward Greensboro on Caspian Lake. The road along the west shore of the lake follows a section of the Bayley-Hazen Military road, a Revolutionary War project that stretches from the town of Newbury on the Connecticut River to Hazen's Notch in Westfield. Although the road never reached its ultimate goal—the Canadian border—it did play a crucial role in

Above: For 50 years, scholars, writers and professors in the Northeast have made Caspian Lake their summer retreat.
Right: *Calais.*

opening the northeastern region of the state to settlement. The older towns here, such as Danville, Peacham and Hardwick, lay along the military road.

The young Continental Congress authorized the construction of the road in May of 1776, just two months before the Declaration of Independence was signed. Supposedly the brainchild of General George Washington, who believed it would "facilitate the march and the return of troops in that quarter," the idea was actually proposed to the general by Jacob Bayley, Newbury settler and granteer. Bayley knew that a road through the wilderness would attract and hasten settlement in the region, and Newbury, as the jump-off point for the road, would prosper. Bayley also had holdings in the unsettled territory to the north, and he stood to gain personally from an influx of pioneers. At the time Bayley made his pro-

posal to General Washington in April 1776, no settlements existed between Newbury and Swanton on Lake Champlain.

Bayley convince Washington that the road would enable American troops to reach St. John, Quebec without going through the Champlain Valley. They might thus gain control of this part of Canada. However, after only a few months of construction, work stopped because Benedict Arnold's invasion of Canada up the Champlain Valley had failed, and the military feared that the finished road would be a fine route by which the British could invade northern New England.

After the Americans' victory at Saratoga in 1777, visions of an invasion of Canada revived. The road was pushed to Hazen's Notch under the supervision of Moses Hazen—another man with considerable personal interest in its construc-

PETER LEMON PHOTOS BOTH PAGES

Left: The lonely hamlet of South Wheelock.
Far left: Much of the historic Bayley-Hazen Road still is in use.

tion. However, when work ended with the snows of late 1779, the British forces still were strong enough to make completion of the ill-fated road an invitation to disaster. Today nearly two thirds of the 54-mile way are still in use, and maps of the entire route—a true backroads experience—are available from the Northeast Vermont Development Association in Lyndonville.

Greensboro, long a summer haven, draws its faithful back year after year, even generation after generation. In the 1930s, academics and literati of the northeastern U.S. "discovered" Caspian Lake; today it is a quiet summer colony in which Willey's Store—in the center of Greensboro village—functions as the main meeting place for long-time friends and residents.

The road over Stannard Mountain perhaps is most authentically experienced at night, or in thick fog or driving rain. It is long and high and wild, and can seem endless in dim or nonexistent light. It is also more fun that way—or so some diehard backroaders believe. The scenery, in any case, is not the most outstanding feature of this road. Trees and decrepit dwellings and abandoned cars are the major highlights of the landscape.

Be prepared for less-than-ideal road conditions, although the Stannard-to-Wheelock road is certainly passable in dry weather. And beware deceptive turn-offs—they may lead to unfortunate dead ends. At the four corners at South Wheelock, the route turns south to North Danville. The road is still high, the countryside still lonely and predominantly wooded, although farms and fields become more common near North Danville. The route crosses the Sleepers River at North Danville, then curves west and south to the main village of Danville.

DICK DIETRICH

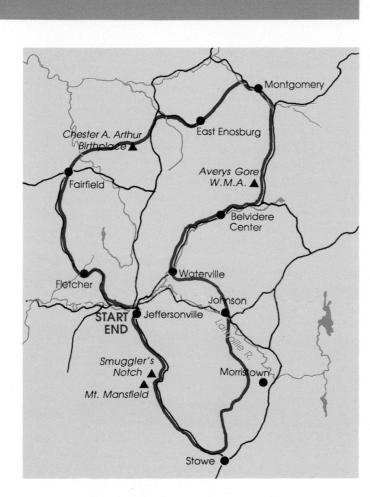

GEORGE WUERTHNER

Through Smuggler's Notch, Johnson, Montgomery, Fairfield

Vermont sprouts mountains—to varying degrees—in almost every corner. Hills and knobs are commonplace and, among the Taconics, the isolated granite protrusions of the Northeast Kingdom and the summits of the Green Mountain Range from Camel's Hump south, are prominences truly wor-

thy of the designation "mountain." Mt. Mansfield, however, is a little bit more.

At 4,393' above sea level, it is the highest point in Vermont. But elevation alone does not explain the difference— one of kind more than degree—between Mt. Mansfield and other summits in the state. Standing along the Lamoille River near Jeffersonville, on an early spring day, one can begin to see what makes Mansfield unique in Vermont.

The bottomland fields are already a soft emerald, and the trees have turned a pale chartreuse, preparing to fountain into leafy green. In contrast to this fertile and greening valley, Mt. Mansfield soars into the clouds southeast of Jeffersonville, still mantled by a cloak of snow. From this angle, the top third

Above: Mt. Mansfield.

Facing page: Waterville and the North Branch of the Lamoille River.

"Hunter and his dog" in Smuggler's Notch—chiseled out by glacial ice.

of the massif seems like a blunt blade, axing into the clouds. Later in the season, when the trees on the mountain slopes leaf out, the most striking difference between this peak and all others in the state will be evident. On Mansfield, the trees do not reach to the top. Other mountains possess small patches of alpine tundra—that zone above treeline—but Mansfield's is by far the most extensive. In a state where most mountains are green all the way to their summits, Mt. Mansfield is uniquely alpine in its appearance, geology and ecology.

Southeast on Route 108 from Jeffersonville to Smuggler's Notch, the encircling walls of a broad amphitheater of mountains reach out to enclose the valley of the Brewster River. At the head of this basin, where the Smuggler's Notch ski area and accompanying developments cluster, the road begins to climb steeply. During the Ice Ages, glacial ice probably funnelled into the basin, then squeezed into the Notch—originally incised by streams into the Green Mountain massif. The ice gouged the striking defile bounded by high, rocky cliffs. At its maximum advance, the glaciers probably overrode the crest of Mansfield itself, planing the northwest side of the mountain and plucking rocks from the subsequently steepened southeast side. Mansfield's height, as well as its geographic location—which exposed it to the full force of advancing glaciers—explains its sharp, glacially sculpted features.

The 250 acres of alpine tundra atop Mt. Mansfield harbor many rare or endangered plants. Several hiking trails as well as a summit toll road lead to this intriguing piece of Vermont, where plant and animal life has adapted to extremely harsh conditions: cold, wind, lack of moisture, heavy snow cover in winter, frost-free growing season of 90 days or less. In fact, a good number of the plants found here are similar to, or the same as, species found in the Arctic: alpine bilberry, Bigelow's sedge, black crowberry and mountain cranberry.

The rugged cliffs within Smuggler's Notch host another kind of arctic flora, but one adapted to climatic conditions distinctly different from those on Mansfield's summit. The rock walls lie mostly in shadow, so plants growing on them remain cool and moist throughout the summer—when lack of moisture stresses the vegetation exposed to wind and light atop Mt. Mansfield. In winter, little snow accumulates on these vertical faces, while it piles deep on the horizontal ridges and gentler mountain slopes. Thus the cliff plants endure ice and more extreme winter temperatures than the snow-insulated mountaintop plants. Among the plant species tucked into craggy pockets of the Notch are purple mountain saxifrage and the carnivorous butterwort, which captures insects with its sticky leaves.

Smuggler's Notch earned its name before the War of 1812, when this area, like Saint Albans, reacted to President Jefferson's embargo on trade with Canada by disobeying it. At that time, only a trail traversed the remote pass. Even today, travel through the Notch is something of an adventure. The extremely steep and winding road accommodates traffic only between the end of May and the end of November. (For those embarking on this backroads tour in early spring or late fall, be sure to check with a reliable source before heading up to the Notch.)

Descending the eastern slopes of the Green Mountains, Route 108 passes the Stowe ski area and accompanying developments that cater to skiers and tourists. The village of Stowe itself is a bustling, congested hub of activity almost any time of year. Although no longer Vermont's largest ski area, Stowe remains the ski capital of the East and a first-class year round resort.

The route through Smuggler's Notch, although wild and dramatic, cannot be termed a true backroads experience. But heading north from the village of Stowe, on a hilltop road that affords fine views of the Worcester Range to the east and uplands northeast of Johnson, travelers can truly feel "off the beaten path." Signs of the wealth that Stowe attracts are prominent for the first several miles beyond the village. Well kept old homes, along with expensive, sometimes fanciful modern structures, sit back among the trees. The byway turns to dirt, climbing, then eventually dips down to cross Sterling Brook via a covered bridge. The way remains mostly woodsy through Morristown. Near the village of Johnson, the road spans roiling Hill Brook, which plunges through a narrow gorge en route to the Lamoille River.

Where the route meets the Lamoille, the stream slips across giant boulders into a broad, flatwater pool. The river eddies several times before rushing again on its course to Lake Champlain. The route parallels the river for a mile, then crosses into Johnson—an attractive, busy village and home to Johnson State College. The road to the college rises onto hills overlooking the Lamoille River valley and affords views of the mountains to the south. From here, a dirt road leads to the village of Waterville, and intersects the Long Trail about half-way there.

The mineral talc is was mined in Johnson as it was at several other Vermont localities, including Chester, Cavendish and West Windsor. The Johnson mine opened around 1908; a mill also was built in the village. Vermont talc was purportedly the "smoothest and softest of any produced in this country" at the time. By 1916, Vermont was a leading talc producer, second only to New York state. In 1983, Vermont led the nation in producing this mineral used in a wide variety of products and manufacturing processes, including bond paper, paints and varnishes, automobile tires, talc crayons and scented powder.

Another important mineral still is mined at Belvidere Mountain, on the townline between Belvidere and Lowell. Asbestos, discovered there in 1893, prompted a kind of asbestos "boom" by 1906. Plenty of speculators responded to the new use of the material in automobile brake linings. But the mines struggled until 1930 when a new corporation took over. That same year the mines produced 83 percent of the asbestos mined in the U.S. Today, Belvidere Mountain accounts for 90 percent of U.S. production. Nonetheless, domestic supplies of

DICK DIETRICH

asbestos fill only some 10 percent of domestic demand. Canadian asbestos, from the huge deposits in Quebec, covers the other 90 percent used in the manufacture of shingles, siding, roofing, cement,building board, paper, felt and pipe coverings.

From Waterville to Montgomery, the land takes on a decidedly "northern" look. The mountain ridges coalesce into more-isolated knobs and humps. Steep and rocky Laraway Mountain dominates the scenery from Waterville to Belvidere Center, but to the east the valley of the North Branch of the Lamoille widens into a nearly uninhabited basin, carpeted with pointy spruces and extensive wetland. This refreshing

The Worcester Range, a subsidiary range east of the Green Mountains, is visible from hills above Stowe.

93

but brief broad space ends as the route leaves Route 109 for Route 118 to Montgomery Center. The narrow passage between the Cold Hollow Mountains and the main Green Mountain chain skirts Averys Gore Wildlife Management Area and passes a shady roadside picnic area on the South Branch of the Trout River. (A "gore" is a piece of land left over after town boundaries were inaccurately surveyed. There are two other gores in Vermont.)

The town of Montgomery boasts six covered bridges, five of them only a short distance off Route 118. The sixth sits on a byway southwest of the main village. Montgomery itself is one of the most attractive communities in this part of the state, encircled by steep hills and graced by well preserved structures including the 1835 church that now houses the town's historical museum.

The route turns off Route 118 just north of the village and crosses the Trout River by means of one of Montgomery's covered bridges. As the road, once again unpaved and remote, climbs to the crest of the northern Cold Hollow Mountains, it dramatically displays the impressive summits of the northern Green Mountain Range to the east. Many higher peaks at this end of the range demonstrate the work of glaciers with typical "sheepback" profiles. The northern slopes are gradual and smooth, but the southern sides of these mountains are abrupt, steep and rocky where ice plucked materials away from the slopes.

The upland ride through Enosburg travels through poor farm country and forested hills; most of the town's population and economic activity is concentrated along the Missisquoi River at Enosburg Falls. At the crossroads in East Enosburg, the paved fork leads to West Enosburg and Route 108 for about a mile and a half, to the turn-off to Bordoville and President Chester A. Arthur's birthplace.

The 21st president was born in 1830, son of a Baptist minister. Arthur's birthplace and original homestead are replicated in the 1953 structure that stands at the site today, furnished with mementoes of his boyhood.

The ambitious northern Vermonter was a school teacher and lawyer before entering New York City politics in the late 1860s. During his term as the head of the city's customs house, an investigation into the operations and personnel of his administration revealed rampant corruption, graft and incompetency. Although personally an honest man, Arthur closed his eyes to unethical doings around him. He was removed from his appointment, but later rose again during the Republican presidential convention of 1880, where he was nominated as the party's vice-presidential candidate. He shared the winning ticket with James Garfield. In July of the following year, an assassin shot Garfield, who died two months later. The country was stunned to find the "Gentleman Boss" its top executive.

But honesty and competent management marked Chester Arthur's administration, much to the surprise of friends and foes alike. He was, however, thwarted throughout his term by an uncooperative Congress, and a political blunder late in his term dealt a fatal blow to his chances for the presidential nomination in 1884.

Enosburg and Fairfield both lie within Franklin County, Vermont's leading dairy county. The prominence of the grange hall in Fairfield village testifies to the enduring importance of agriculture in this region, which supports the highest density of cows in Vermont—61 per square mile in 1982.

The road leading south of Fairfield climbs into rockier, less-fertile hills. Fletcher, along with the neighboring town of Bakersfield, records the lowest cow density in this dairy county—25 per square mile. Although Fletcher's soil has proved poor, it is wealthy in scenic beauty, and claims some of the most dramatic views in the state. Mt. Mansfield is the centerpiece of broad panoramas available from the hills of Fletcher; from here, the mountain looks enormous.

Following the paved way back to the Lamoille River, the tour route meets Route 104 just east of the pretty village of Cambridge, a couple miles to the tour's starting point at Jeffersonville.

NORTHEAST KINGDOM

GEORGE WUERTHNER

96

THROUGH THE NORTHEAST CORNER
OF VERMONT

Land of spruce bogs, moose and few humans, this region was aptly named by Senator George Aiken in 1949 when he declared to a gathering in Lyndonville, "You know, this is such beautiful country up here. It ought to be called the Northeast Kingdom of Vermont."

The remote northeast corner of the state, taking in Essex, Caledonia and Orleans counties, always has seemed a world apart. To this day it remains the wildest and least-known part of Vermont. Long after Ohio and much of the Midwest had been settled, towns in the Northeast Kingdom had yet to see a single inhabitant. Some towns, like Lewis in Essex County, have never had one human resident, and the region as a whole accounts for less than 10 percent of Vermont's population, although it takes up almost one fifth of its area.

The region's thin, acidic soils and particularly harsh climate discouraged settlement and tested the endurance of the few hardy pioneers that came here. No large body of water ameliorates the extremes of temperature, as Lake Champlain does on the west side of the state. Bloomfield, on the Connecticut River, claims both the Vermont and New England record low temperature of -50° F.

The Kingdom's generally high land can be observed from the village of Brownington, or the road from Guildhall to Granby. An extension of the White Mountain granite complex, its hard rocks resist erosion. The scattered peaks and knobs that protrude from the rolling surface of the highlands are monadnocks—like Mount Ascutney in Windsor County.

The northeast corner of Vermont is also very wet. Ice Age glaciers not only carved out depressions in the bedrock to become beautiful lakes like Lake Willoughby and Lake Seymour. They also left huge quantities of glacial sediment that hinder drainage and have thus left the Kingdom typically boggy, swampy and untillable ground.

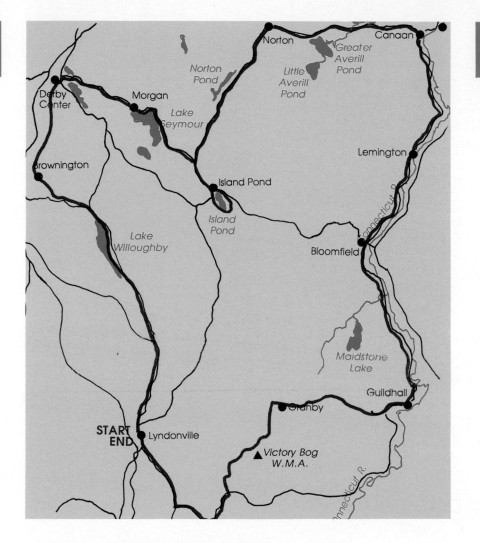

Poor hsoils, poor climate, and—until recent times—its distance from urban areas, combined to make the Northeast Kingdom the most economically depressed part of Vermont. However, the region has always been wealthy in trees, and the lumber industry and related manufacturing have sustained the people of the Kingdom, Essex County in particular, since the earliest days of its settlement. Private timber companies, in fact, own much of the acreage in Essex, as well as parts of Caledonia and Orleans. Champion International, Vermont's

Facing page: Paper birch along the shore of Lake Willoughby—a fine example of glacial carving.

GEORGE WUERTHNER

largest private landowner, owns 225,000 acres of timberland, most of it in the Northeast Kingdom.

The tour begins at Lyndonville, a venerable and attractive community settled relatively early for the region, well situated as it is on the lowlands along the Passumpsic River. The town of Lyndon operates as a service and trade center for less-populated areas to the north. The campus of Lyndon State College here commands a superb view of the Passumpsic Valley and Burke Mountain. Lyndonville also can be considered the birthplace of AT&T. Theodore Vail, company founder, had a summer residence here, and it was during one of his visits to this northern Vermont village that he formulated his ideas for a national, as well as international, telecommunications system.

Route 5 heads north out of Lyndonville for West Burke, from where Route 5A should then be followed to Lake Willoughby. Although not a true backroad, this scenic drive through the classic, glacially-sculpted valley between the dark cliffs of Mount Pisgah and Mount Hor, is not to be missed. As with the Finger Lakes of New York, this long, glacial ice carved narrow and deep Lake Willoughby—probably exploiting a pre-existing depression or zone of weakness in the hard bedrock. The valley's U shape, with a gently-sloping-to-almost-flat valley bottom and steep sidewalls, is the signature of a glacier. From the summit of Mount Pisgah (at 2,751' above sea level) to Willoughby's bottom is a span of more than 3,000'—making Lake Willougby one of the deepest lakes in New England.

Arctic flora like that in Smuggler's Notch can be found on the cliffs of Mount Pisgah. Trails lead to the top of this peak as well as 2,648' Mount Hor. A rare bird may soon make its home on Willoughby's cliffs again. In recent years conservationinsts have tried to restore the endangered peregrine falcon to the state, after an absence of some three decades. At one time 40 peregrine eyries were documented throughout Vermont. The last active eyrie in the state was on the cliffs above Willoughby, but since 1950 no peregrines have nested here. The demise of this swift-flying predator throughout its range was due mainly to the widespread use of the pesticide DDT, which poisoned the birds and damaged their reproductive systems. The restoration effort is part of a nation-wide campaign to bring back the peregrine. The native Northeast-

GEORGE WUERTHNER

PETER LEMON

Left: *Lake Seymour, Morgan.*
Far left: *The Old Stone House in Brownington, where the Orleans Historical Society maintains a small museum.*

Facing page: *Essex County is rich in timber, moose and bogs, but poor in economic opportunities.*

ern subspecies is apparently extinct, but the young of a very similar subspecies are being introduced at Lake Willoughby and other locations in the state.

The elegant community of Brownington perches atop a broad, open hill, surrounded by distant views in every direction. The settlement's most interesting feature, the Old Stone House, contains the collections of the Orleans Historical Society, and is itself a fascinating attraction. Alexander Twilight constructed the granite building between 1827 and 1829 as an "Athenian Hall" to bring learning and knowledge to the north-country farm children. It is reminiscent of the early dorms on the Middlebury College campus. Twilight was purportedly an 1823 Middlebury graduate, and the first black to graduate from an American college.

The wooden observatory tower on Prospect Hill, in Brownington, is maintained by the Vermont Division of Historical Preservation and offers a 360° panorama of the Kingdom. Lake Memphremagog reclines to the north, Jay Peak to the west, and the distinctive humps of Mt. Hor and Mt. Pisgah are silhouetted against the eastern horizon.

A dirt road descends to Derby town and the junction of Routes 105 and 111. The latter highway heads east for Lake Seymour in the town of Morgan. Seymour is the second-largest body of water wholly contained within Vermont's borders, after Lake Bomoseen. Although most of its shore is privately

owned, a small strip of beach adjoining the road provides a place for visitors to reach the water.

Before continuing north on Route 114 to Norton and Averill on the Canadian border, travelers should devote 45 minutes or so to making a side trip to the lakeshore village of Island Pond. In the latter part of the 19th century this was a busy stop on the Portland-to-Montreal Grand Trunk railroad. The large depot and spacious downtown bear silent witness to former days of glory. Today Island Pond is better known as the earthly home of a religious cult that moved here from Tennessee in 1978; the women of the Northeast Kingdom Community Church cover their heads in long scarves, the men typically are bearded.

The village is best viewed from the south end of the pond. A loop drive around it passes Brighton State Park, which offers beach access to both Island and Spectacle ponds.

En route to Norton, the route passes through Warren Gore—an odd tract of land chartered with the town of Warren (in Washington County) so that the latter contained enough acreage to legally comprise a town. This "flying grant," as it was called, never had a permanent resident until 1970, when the census revealed one person. The Gore's neighbor to the west, Warner's Grant, has been similarly uninhabited since the state bequeathed it to the widow of Green Mountain Boy Seth Warner. Left destitute after her husband's

The upper stretches of the Connecticut River are desolate and tranquil, unlike its southern reaches. Near Guildhall.

death, Hester Warner petitioned the Vermont legislature for a grant of land with which to support herself and her three children. By that time—1787—much of Vermont was already granted. When Hester at last received her 2,000 acres in the remote northeast corner of the state, one can only hope she had found another means of sustaining her family.

The lonely town of Norton was not settled until 1860. For several decades afterwards, it is said, there was no road leading out of Norton into Vermont, except by way of Canada. Where Route 114 turns sharply east, travelers can look into the province of Quebec, and observant ones will note the red "Arret" along with the English "Stop" signs at this end of the state. French-speaking Canadian tourists frequently travel into Vermont, and people of French-Canadian heritage make up about one third of the communities on the northern border of the state.

French Canadians comprise probably the largest immigrant ethnic group to arrive in the state after the first wave of American colonial settlers in the late 18th century. The first migration of French Canadians occurred before 1830, and another wave swept in after 1840. Both were largely urban movements, although the majority of immigrants had farmed in Quebec. Some of them eventually did acquire farms in the Green Mountain State. The third wave of immigration occurred after 1880. Again, although most immigrants worked in mills and factories in the towns and cities, most of them wanted farmland. With the hinterlands emptying of native Vermont farm boys and girls, these newcomers were able to move onto their rocky farms.

Great Averill Pond, a glacially scoured basin, features a wonderfully underdeveloped, semi-wild lake. A few well kept cottages line its shores, but it is for the most part a quiet place to picnic, fish or canoe.

Route 114 continues to Canaan, where a branch plant of the Ethan Allen Furniture Company employs some 500 people in a town of 1,200. The clearcuts visible from the highway indicate the importance of the timber and wood products industry to this region. The Ethan Allen Company, the largest single employer in the northeast corner of the state, operates two other plants at Orleans and Brighton. The three Northeast Kingdom counties lead the state's annual cut of sawlogs. Essex is far and away the king of pulpwood—some 122,093 boardfeet per square mile were cut here in 1984, compared to runner-up Caledonia's 59,007 board feet per square mile. The region long has been an important producer of pulpwood because of its wealth of spruce—the only species the limited papermaking technology of the 1880s could utilize.

Trivia buffs and other aficionados of useless peculiarities should take an interesting side trip to the northeasternmost corner of Vermont. By simply paralleling the Connecticut River (here really just a broad stream) a mile and a half past Beecher Falls one will reach a stone boundary marker that designates the dividing line between Vermont and New Hampshire. On a map, it looks as if the Green Mountain State is poking a narrow finger into the White Mountain State, as New Hampshire is not only the eastern, but also the northern neighbor to this piece of Vermont.

The northern valley of the Connecticut is fairly narrow but in some ways more dramatic than the lower river valley. Here, precipitous mountain slopes rise from the water on the New Hampshire side; dense, uninhabited woods reach westward from Route 102 on the Vermont side. At Bloomfield the desolate highway finally intersects another major road—Route 105 from Island Pond. The Nulhegan River also reaches the end of its course through lonely timberlands here.

It was probably with great relief that a contingent of Major Robert Rogers' soldiers—better known as Rogers' Rangers—arrived at this point in 1759. They had been sent by General Jeffrey Amherst (commander at the Crown Point fort on Lake Champlain) to attack an Indian village in Canada. After successfully laying waste to the village, Rogers and his men were to return south via Lake Memphremagog and the Nulhegan to the Connecticut, whence they would proceed to Fort Number 4 at the eastern terminus of the Crown Point Road.

After the attack on the Indian village, the French and their Indian allies pursued the Rangers all the way to Memphremagog. Suffering from lack of supplies and wounds inflicted by their pursuers, the group split at Lake Memphremagog, half continuing along the pre-designated route, the other heading more directly through the present-day towns of Victory and Granby. By the time they rendezvoused at Newbury on the Connecticut, where they expected to find a resupply cache, the goods had been shipped back down the river. They also had lost half of their men. Weak from starvation, the Rangers struggled into Fort Number 4—a month and a half after they had set off from Crown Point.

The town of Brunswick made its bid for posh resort status in the late 1860s, when A.J. Congden of Lancaster, New Hampshire bought and promoted the Brunswick Springs. Six separate springs flowed from a bank above the Connecticut River at that time, and Congden shrewdly (though rather unscientifically) designated them Iron Spring, Calcium Spring, Magnesium, White Sulphur, Bromine and Arsenic springs. Health-seekers were to mix these waters in specific amounts to achieve the perfect remedy for whatever ailed them. The gimmick was popular, if not medically effective, and Congden's resort flourished for a time.

The road to Maidstone State Forest turns off Route 102 about 4 to 5 miles south of the crossroads at Bloomfield. This deep, publicly accessible lake supports lake trout, landlocked salmon and smelt and, occasionally, loon and moose are seen here. Perhaps even more interesting than the lake itself is the ground surrounding it, covered with a heavy layer of glacial deposits—boulders, gravel and sand.

Guildhall is the last haven of elegance and civility before the route plunges into the wildest stretch of the tour, through the towns of Granby and Victory. Plain but dignified homes and public buildings rim a spacious, tree-shaded green. The only exception, a lemon-yellow structure with stained glass windows and trim that make it look like a birthday cake, serves as the public library.

A signed road turns off Route 102 about 2 miles beyond Guildhall. The town of Granby is so remote that it did not receive electricity until 1963. About 125 people dwell in the rough hills and along the stream bottoms of Granby and Victory, but most of this area provides better habitat for moose than for humans.

In recent years the private timber companies that hold much of the acreage in these two towns, as well as other parts of the Northeast Kingdom, have indicated that they will transfer their operations in the near future. With the prospect of huge tracts of wild land coming up for bid, conservationists as well as government agencies are beginning to realize that this is a unique opportunity to acquire desperately needed public land for the crowded populace of the Northeast U.S.

The broad Guildhall town common.

The proposal for a Northeast Kingdom National Park and Recreation Area, although controversial, is being discussed in ever-widening circles, and offers the possibility of finally bringing prosperity to this perennially depressed region.

Preservation of the wild Northeast Kingdom also offers the possibility of bringing back a wealth of wildlife that once was here, but was seriously depleted by settlement, land clearing and overhunting. One species already tentatively recolonizing the state is the moose. It was driven out by land clearing in the 19th century, but today numbers between 25 and 50 individuals. Moose face several roadblocks to their recovery in Vermont, however, the most significant created by humans. While moose die every year from a parasitic brain worm that may induce atypical behavior (like "courting" domestic cows or wandering down the main streets of villages), far more die from automobiles and illegal hunting. Spreading development in the Northeast Kingdom, as well as other parts of the state, hurts the moose's chances of full recovery.

To complete the loop and return to the starting point at Lyndonville, travelers can follow Route 2 for about 7 miles to a paved turnoff that heads north through rural countryside and reaches Lyndonville approximately 7 seven miles farther. An interesting final diversion, the town of Saint Johnsbury, exhibits exemplary Victorian architecture and the Fairbanks Museum and Athenæum. From there, Route 5 follows the Passumpsic River back to Lyndonville.

BOOKS

The Vermont Atlas and Gazetteer, William Hancock, *et al.* De-Lorme Mapping Company, 1978.

The Nature of Vermont, Charles W. Johnson. University Press of New England, Hanover, NH, 1980, third printing 1984.

Vermont's Land and Resources, Harold Meeks. The New England Press, Shelburne, VT, 1986.

Time and Change in Vermont: A Human Geography, Harold Meeks. The Globe Pequot Press, Chester, CT, 1986.

Vermont: A History, Charles Morrisey. W.W. Norton, NY, 1984, 1981.

Vermont Place-Names: Footprints of History, Esther Swift. The Stephen Green Press, Brattleboro, VT, 1977.

Roadside Geology of Vermont and New Hampshire, Bradford B. Van Diver. Mountain Press, Missoula, MT 1987.

AGENCIES AND ORGANIZATIONS

Vermont Travel Division, 134 State Street, Montpelier, 05602.

Vermont Dept. of Forests, Parks, and Recreation, Waterbury, 05676.

Vermont Dept. of Fish and Wildlife, Waterbury, 05676.

Green Mountain National Forest, P.O. Box 519, Rutland, 05701.

Green Mountain Club, P.O. Box 889, 43 State Street, Montpelier, 05602.

Left: *A sugarhouse near Newark.*
Facing page: *Autumn tints the maples around a West Barnet sugarhouse.*

DICK DIETRICH PHOTOS BOTH PAGES

103

AMERICAN GEOGRAPHIC PUBLISHING

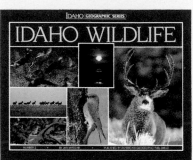

EACH BOOK HAS
ABOUT 100
PAGES, 11" X 8¹/₂",
120 TO 170
COLOR PHOTO-
GRAPHS

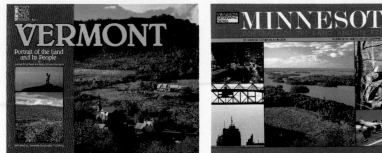

Enjoy, See, Understand America State by State

**American Geographic Publishing
Geographic Series of the States**

Lively, colorful, beautifully illustrated books specially written for these series explain land form, animals and plants, economy, lifestyle and history of each state or feature. Generous color photography brings each state to life and makes each book a treat to turn to frequently. The geographic series format is designed to give you more information than coffee-table photo books, yet so much more color photography than simple guide books.

Each book includes:
- Colorful maps
- Valuable descriptions and charts of features such as volcanoes and glaciers
- Up-to-date understanding of environmental problems where man and nature are in conflict
- References for additional reading, agencies and offices to contact for more information
- Special sections portraying people in their homes, at work, in the countryside

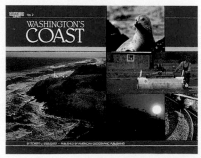

for more information write:
**American Geographic Publishing
P.O. Box 5630
Helena, Montana 59604**